VISITORS' HISTORIC BRITAIN

NORTHUMBERLAND

ROMANS TO VICTORIANS

VISITORS' HISTORIC BRITAIN

NORTHUMBERLAND

ROMANS TO VICTORIANS

CRAIG ARMSTRONG

PEN & SWORD
HISTORY

AN IMPRINT OF PEN & SWORD BOOKS LTD.
YORKSHIRE - PHILADELPHIA

First published in Great Britain in 2020 by
Pen & Sword History
An imprint of
Pen & Sword Books Ltd
Yorkshire – Philadelphia

ISBN 978 1 52670 278 4

A CIP catalogue record for this book is
available from the British Library.

Printed and bound in England
By CPI Group (UK) Ltd, Croydon, CR0 4YY.
Typeset by Aura Technology and Software Services, India.

Pen & Sword Books Limited incorporates the imprints of Atlas, Archaeology,
Aviation, Discovery, Family History, Fiction, History, Maritime, Military, Military
Classics, Politics, Select, Transport, True Crime, Air World, Frontline Publishing, Leo
Cooper, Remember When, Seaforth Publishing, The Praetorian Press, Wharncliffe
Local History, Wharncliffe Transport, Wharncliffe True Crime and White Owl.

For a complete list of Pen & Sword titles please contact

PEN & SWORD BOOKS LIMITED
47 Church Street, Barnsley, South Yorkshire, S70 2AS, England
E-mail: enquiries@pen-and-sword.co.uk
Website: www.pen-and-sword.co.uk

Or
PEN AND SWORD BOOKS
1950 Lawrence Rd, Havertown, PA 19083, USA
E-mail: Uspen-and-sword@casematepublishers.com
Website: www.penandswordbooks.com

To my parents, who gave me a love of Northumberland.

Contents

Introduction

Northumberland is incredibly rich in heritage and history. The county has been a powerful kingdom; a centre of learning; the cradle of Christianity in England; the edge of the Roman Empire; a county which changed hands between England and Scotland; the bastion of England during the Anglo-Scottish Wars of Independence; part of the land which was home to the border reivers; a cradle of the agricultural and industrial revolutions, and a training ground for the British Army and its allies.

Northumberland is now a predominantly rural, peaceful, county renowned for having more castles than any other county in Britain, for its fabulously dramatic scenery and for its beautiful and unspoilt coastline. As of June 2017 the population of Northumberland was just 319,030, meaning that it is one of the least populated counties in Britain with an average population density of just sixty-four people per square kilometre, compared to a national average of 427 and a north-east average of 308.

During the eighteenth and nineteenth centuries especially, the county was home to many entrepreneurs who went on to have impressive careers which left their mark on society, including the father of the railways, a great weapons designer and farming innovators.

Pre-Roman Northumberland

With the coming of widespread agriculture in the Neolithic Age around 4,000 BC, the lives of those living in what is now Northumberland changed radically. The old and well-established hunter-gatherer system of living was gradually replaced by the growing of crops and the gradual (but not complete) replacement of hunting, with the keeping of domesticated livestock.

We cannot be certain about how the agricultural way of life was adapted, but it was likely to have been a gradual process during the Neolithic Age, developing alongside the complex and intricate ritual and ceremonial world of the Mesolithic Age. As people became more attached to a particular piece of land, concepts such as ownership and place would also have changed.

Some research has been conducted in the beautiful valley of the River Coquet (known as the Lady of Rivers and pronounced Coke-it) which lies in mid-Northumberland and stretches from the border to the coast at historic Warkworth, which has shown that cereals used in the production of both beer and bread were introduced to the valley shortly after 4,000 BC. There is also some evidence for the existence of Neolithic fields in and around Rothbury. The introduction of domesticated beasts such as cattle, goats, pigs and sheep was probably more important in this upland area, and it is likely that these early farmers maintained a mobile lifestyle moving their stock between upland and lowland as the seasons demanded. Even today, surviving aspects of this style of farming can be glimpsed, with sheep being hefted to particular hill-territories and cattle being turned out onto the hills in the summer months.

Lordenshaws

A large and impressive site with an Iron Age hillfort, the remains of round houses, burial mounds and incredible examples of rock art.

Set in the Simonside Hills just south of the village of Rothbury, Lordenshaws requires a short walk but the rewards are well worthwhile. The site is within the boundaries of Northumberland National Park and there is a small car park just off the B6342. The fort is situated just 400 metres from the car park and the climb is not strenuous. Thanks to the Duke of Northumberland, the National Park Authority and the local tenant farmer, visitors are free to wander the site inside the marked access area.

The walk from the car park leads along the remains of a medieval deer park wall, and the site itself contains a wealth of archaeology. The fort is roughly circular, covers approximately 140 metres, has two distinct entrances and is surrounded by a dual defensive ditch. Where it is most complete, in the north, the outer ditch is over 2½ metres deep and 9 metres wide. The inner ditch is less well-preserved and appears to have been shallower than the outer one; it would appear that as the fort was expanded, the inner ditch fell into disuse.

The southern half of the fort contains the remains of several small circular structures which may have been for storage or ceremonial purposes, while there are also the remains of a larger round house. It is impossible to be sure, but it appears that the surviving walls of this house are continuous without any entrance and that it may have been partially sunk into the ground and entered in a similar manner to the pit house (or grubenhaus). The northern part of the fort contains two more round houses and it is likely that there are more concealed beneath the ground.

There are several other outworks scattered around the site suggesting that the fort was continuously restructured as demands changed; the site was clearly used for a substantial period of time. There is also a large rectangular enclosure which features the signs of medieval-period ridge-and-furrow markings, enclosed by an earth and boulder wall. This is obviously a later development and maps from the early nineteenth century label it as a cornfield.

To the north-east of the fort are a number of Bronze Age burial cairns. There were changes in the way the dead were interred at around this time. Elsewhere in the country the dead were placed in long-barrow mounds, but in north-eastern England the dead (or their cremated remains) were interred in earth or stone burial mounds such as those found here. Very often the remains were contained within a stone-lined coffin known as a 'cist', and there are several examples of these cists to be found on the site.

Probably the most notable cairn on the site is just over 100 metres to the north-east of the fort. This cairn has clearly been excavated (probably in the nineteenth century) as a trench cuts across it, but the site itself is impressive as it is constructed on an outcrop which is decorated with an impressive series of 'cup-and-ring' rock art. This is a further demonstration of how the site was in continuous use as the rock art pre-dates the hillfort by at least 1,000 years.

Cup-and-ring marks, or rock art, are features carved into rocks during the Neolithic and Bronze Age and are found throughout the country but are particularly common in Northumberland. The meanings of these markings has been lost, but they remain an impressive link with our prehistoric ancestors. As you walk along the path there are several markers which point the visitor towards some of the most interesting rock art sites. The first is called 'main rock' and this features a wealth of art, although it is clear that the stone has also been quarried (possibly to provide stone for the deer park wall). The second stone that you reach is known as 'horseshoe rock' and shows how the rock art follows the contours of the stone (a common occurrence in Northumberland). The next stone is the aptly named 'channel rock'. This is an unusual rock in several ways: it features a long, enhanced groove, there are numerous (and unusual) cup marks on the vertical face of the rock and there are a number of large cups near the top of the panel; it is most unusual to find such numbers of cups without the usually attendant ring markings in Northumberland. Speculation about the enhanced groove has seen it put forward that this slab may very well have been ceremonial in nature. In total there are over 100 marked rocks on the site.

Directions (NZ 05491 99223)
Car – just off the B6342 south of Rothbury. (Sat-Nav: NE61 4PU)
Bus – Arriva service X14 runs regularly to Rothbury from Newcastle but there is a considerable walk involved to reach Lordenshaws from here.

Admission
Free

Facilities

There is a small parking area but otherwise there are no facilities at the site itself. Accommodation can be found in the nearby village of Rothbury which has several hotels and guesthouses including the Turk's Head Hotel [https://www.turksheadrothbury.co.uk], the Queen's Head Hotel [http://www.queensheadrothbury.com], and the Coquetvale Hotel [http://coquetvale.co.uk].

Opening Times

See Northumberland National Park website [https://www.northumberland nationalpark.org.uk/places-to-visit/coquetdale/lordenshaws/]

The Votadini

The first people in Northumberland about whom we know anything with any great certainty were a Brythonic Celtic people believed to have migrated from mainland Europe in around 8 BC. The tribe which seems to have dominated the area now known as Northumberland were the Votadini, although it is probable that the southernmost parts of the county would have been in the territory of the Brigantes. The Votadini territory was easily recognised by the presence of their farms which were frequently surrounded by walls, banks and ditches. It would also seem that the Votadini people did not wear large ornate armlets like many neighbouring tribes, but did make frequent offerings of metal objects. In addition to farms and scattered hamlets, the Votadini also made use of large hillforts across their territory. Some of the largest of these were at Yeavering Bell and Lordenshaws. The hillforts themselves are something of a mystery as many of them would have been difficult to defend, despite their extensive earthwork defences, and it has been speculated that some or all of the hillforts were in fact used primarily for religious and politically significant occasions.

Yeavering Bell stands in the far north of Northumberland on the edge of the Cheviot Hills range near the River Glen valley. It is a twin-peaked hill which stands 361 metres above sea level. It is a wild spot, but well worth the trek to the summit to see the breathtaking remains of one of the most important Iron Age hillforts in the country.

View NE from atop Yeavering Bell (Richard Webb / Walls, Yeavering Bell / CC BY-SA 2.0)

The fort itself spans some 12 acres and is surrounded by a large and impressive stone wall, which is over 3 metres wide in many places and would have stood at 2½ metres in height. The wall is penetrated by four separate entrances and the main entrance, which lines up precisely with neighbouring Hedgehope Hill, has the remains of a guard post. Within the walls is an oval inner fort with more stone walls. This alignment with Hedgehope Hill means that the residents of the Bell hillfort would have looked out to see the sun at its apogee over Hedgehope Hill at approximately noon. It would appear that the hillfort was built in two separate stages of design and the remains of a large number of roundhouses dot the interior. These have caused speculation over whether they indicate that some form of communal living was taking place on the hill, or if they had some other purpose and the site was largely ceremonial. The sides of the hill also have large numbers of roundhouse remains, as does the valley between Yeavering Bell and the neighbouring Whitelaw Hill. Once again, there are archaeological variations in these remains with some houses being grouped behind rudimentary ramparts while others stand alone. The sides of the hill also have a number of burial barrows hinting at further ceremonial and/or religious importance. Archaeologists have also established that most of the defences were constructed from locally available andesite which would, when first quarried, have been a light pink colour, fading with age to the dull grey that we see today. Thus, the fort on Yeavering Bell would certainly have stood out at some distance, increasing speculation that these hillforts played a role in advertising and marking territorial boundaries or important ritual locations.

As well as the archaeological and heritage sites at Yeavering Bell, a visitor who takes the time to make the journey to the top of the hill might just be lucky enough to see some of the wild goats which graze in the area. Although these goats are not native, they were introduced during the Neolithic period and the remaining herds, Northumberland is one of the few strongholds left in Britain, are descended from domesticated animals which were replaced by sheep during the Middle Ages. They are a hardy and agile beast with a distinct herd structure.

CHAPTER 1

The Romans

The majority of what would become Northumberland had been under Roman rule or influence for approximately 350 years and this had brought many changes to the area and its inhabitants. The Romans brought with them foreign soldiers who went on to settle in the area while roads, forts and towns all resulted in improved communications and trading opportunities. During the reign of Emperor Constantine the Great (he was named as Emperor at York), the Romans also introduced Christianity to the area. We do not know with any certainty how the native people adapted to the new religion as it was merely one of many which were permitted in the Empire; it is possible that the vast majority of people carried on worshipping the same deities as before. Language also changed; the native Celtic tongue (probably similar to Welsh) continued to dominate among the native Britons, but with the Romans came the introduction of Latin, while their foreign soldiers brought other languages, most notably Germanic.

The Romans invaded Britain in AD 43 and we know that three years later the Brigantes tribe (who inhabited vast lands stretching from Southern Yorkshire to north of the River Tyne) had become a client state of the invaders. While they had not been actively conquered it would seem that, like others, the Brigantes, under their ruling queen, Cartimandua, had decided to submit to the Romans in the hope that it would see them spared invasion and possibly benefit from increased trade.

Some eight years later, however, Cartimandua divorced her husband, Venutius, and a rift developed between the Roman-supporting queen and her former husband, who advocated resistance against the invaders. After five years the Romans responded to the growing rebellion by conquering the Brigantes and Venutius. The persistent Venutius survived this reverse and by 69 he had forced his former wife from the north and become leader of the Brigantes. Two years later, the Brigantes were in open rebellion with a series of battles being fought against the Romans. In AD 71, however, the rebellion ended when a Roman force defeated Venutius and his Brigantes.

This was not the end of resistance in the north; throughout the next five decades revolts among the northern tribes were commonplace enough to concern the Emperor Hadrian. The Emperor visited the area in AD 121 and ordered the building of a massive wall to separate Roman Britain from the northern barbarians, and also to split the rebellious tribes making it harder for tribes such as the Votadini (who lived in much of what is now Northumberland) to ally with other more southerly tribes such as the Brigantes. The wall was an engineering marvel and, remarkably, was completed within five years.

Over the next forty years Roman occupation see-sawed between Hadrian's Wall and the Antonine Wall in Scotland. During this period the Romans also built a road network in the lands that would one day become Northumberland, and built the first recorded bridge over the River Tyne at what would become Newcastle but which was then known as Pons Aelius. Despite these developments the northern territories remained rebellious. In AD 180 it was reported that another revolt had resulted in the death of a Roman general, and seventeen years later a revolt led by the Maetae tribe across Hadrian's Wall resulted in further bloodshed for the Romans on this bloody frontier.

Given the nature of duty on the wall it seems little wonder that a warriors' god named Mithras became widely worshipped by those who guarded, and lived on, the frontier. At least four temples to Mithras (known as Mithraeum) have been discovered on Hadrian's Wall and it is possible there were more.

The Romans undertook almost continual repairs to the wall and combined this with further offensive operations to try to stamp out the rebellions. In AD 208, a strong Roman force under Emperor Septimus Severus defeated the northern tribes and established a strong system of roads and supply bases in the lands of Northumberland. One of the most noted of these supply bases was created at what is now Corbridge on the River Tyne. The Roman army slaughtered a tribe of native Celts here and established a colony. As relative peace came to the area, life under the Roman invaders became almost normalised and civilian settlements known as 'vici' began to develop around many of the Roman forts in the area. These vici fulfilled an important role in life on the frontier; they were home to craftsmen who sold their goods to the occupiers, merchants who ordered and delivered supplies and luxuries, and women who began to intermarry with the invaders. One of the foremost of these vici was the village which came to be known as Vindolanda and which was first reported around AD 270.

In AD 296 yet another revolt of the northern tribes erupted and, because many soldiers had been withdrawn from Hadrian's Wall due to revolt in Rome itself, the tribes were able to overrun the defences of the wall. Once again, however, the revolt did not last; just a year later the Romans once again began repairs to the forts along the length of the wall. This effort was part of a large-scale Roman effort to improve the defences in the area and significant strengthening of a number of the wall forts, including High Rochester, Risingham and Housesteads was undertaken, along with a significant road building effort.

The improved defences did not seem to help when yet another revolt began in AD 367. It is the largest recorded revolt faced by the Romans in the north and there is evidence that it was very well organised, with Picts, Irish and Scots all working together, along with groups of Germanic pirates. Although the revolt was eventually put down, it marked the beginning of a period of renewed and almost continuous violence. By AD 383 the Roman Empire was under severe pressure from the Goths, and many Roman forces were removed from the increasingly embattled frontier for service on the Continent. As a result, the remaining Romans suffered heavy casualties and were defeated by their enemies, culminating in the decision to order the abandonment of Britain in 399 AD. This process took several years, during which the northern tribes continued the battle against their foes, overrunning much of what is now Northumberland. By AD 410 the Roman evacuation was largely completed and Britain was no longer a part of the teetering Roman Empire.

During the entire Roman period, the majority of the land that is now Northumberland was in a peculiar relationship with the Roman conquerors. While the Empire officially extended only as far as Hadrian's Wall, the vast majority of Northumberland lay to the north and the tribes here would have experienced a mixture of cooperation and hostility towards the Romans.

We know that these northern tribes traded with the Romans, but we also know that they played a full role in the many rebellions that took place. A number of Roman frontier forts can be found in Northumberland proving that the influence of the Roman army extended beyond the wall even.

By the end of Roman rule the native Britons had intermingled with the invaders to such an extent that we now describe them as being Romano-British. Marriage of native Britons to Roman soldiers who could have been drawn from across the Empire furthered this developing multiculturalism. At the impressive fort of Housesteads, for example, we know from the archaeological research of numerous academics and local groups that there was a Roman garrison consisting of Anglo-Saxon soldiers and that there was frequent intermarriage between these Anglo-Saxons and the native population. (See Crow, J. *Housesteads: A Fort and Garrison on Hadrian's Wall* (Tempus: 2004)).

Hadrian's Wall

The wall dominates much of the scenery of southern Northumberland and attracts a large number of tourists. When Hadrian visited Britain in AD 122, he took the decision to abandon the territories to the north of the wall and ordered his governor, Aulus Platorius Nepos, to construct a permanent boundary between the Tyne and the Solway Firth.

The wall was a fantastically demanding project, stretching over 73 miles from Wallsend on the River Tyne to the Solway Firth in Cumbria. The fact that the wall was constructed in stone demonstrates the importance that the Emperor placed upon it. Hadrian had decreed that the Empire would not extend beyond the limits it already had, and thus the wall was as much a demarcation line separating the Empire from the barbarians as it was a defensive feature. However, the wall was also defensible with small forts known as milecastles at every mile, and a number of smaller turrets between these milecastles. The milecastles themselves vary in design as they were constructed by different military units. A number of forts were also built along the wall, while two large ditches were dug to the north and south of the wall. It has been estimated that the wall was originally 15ft high with a 6ft parapet and varied from 8–10ft wide.

The remains of the wall are not continuous, as large portions around Newcastle have been built over and large sections of the wall between Heddon and Shield-on-the-Wall were used as the base for a military road during the eighteenth century. There are sections which still survive, especially where the terrain was too steep for the road builders. The fort of Carrowburgh has survived and is well worth a visit. Other forts at Rudchester and Haltonchesters have not survived in an extant form but the mounds of the structures can still be seen.

A little to the west is the attractive shopping village of Corbridge. The modern village arose from the Roman town of Corstopitum. Originally, the town was named Coria, believed to be a Celtic word meaning hosting place. The town was constructed at an important junction on the north bank of the Tyne and was the site where Dere Street crossed the river; it was thus a vital link in the supply chain that maintained the wall and quickly attracted tradesmen and craftsmen. Corstopitum became a bustling town with a cosmopolitan mix of people, civilians and soldiers. It was also the most northerly town in the Roman Empire.

Corbridge Museum and Corstopitum

Visitors can walk around the streets of the ancient town, while the museum holds probably the most important and largest collection of artefacts discovered on the wall. The Corbridge hoard was discovered in 1964 when a buried iron-shod leather chest was discovered by archaeologists. The chest contained a 2,000-year-old time capsule in excellent condition. The hoard included the equipment of a Roman soldier and many of the contents of a Roman workshop. The find stunned historians and archaeologists and its state of preservation and completeness allowed experts to discover more about how Roman armour was constructed. There had been much debate over how the equipment came to be buried in the chest, with many believing that its owner probably buried the equipment to be recovered afterwards but failed to return (possibly as a result of one of the many revolts).

The museum houses approximately 34,000 artefacts and is the largest Hadrian's Wall collection to be managed by English Heritage. The many inscriptions, religious dedications and building inscriptions provide great

Corbridge Roman Ruins (Glen Bowman CC BY 2.0 https://en.wikipedia.org/wiki/ Coria_(Corbridge)#/media/File:Corbridge_Roman_Ruins.jpg)

depth and scope in their range. They include dedications to deities from across the Roman Empire while many names of units and individual soldiers who had been stationed at or near Corbridge are also to be found. One of the reasons the collections is so interesting is that many of the artefacts show the civilian side of life on the Roman frontier. There are collections of objects which belonged to women, such as hairpins for example, and items which give an insight into the lives of both civilians and off-duty soldiers such as a gaming board with counters, dice and shaker.

Five lion statues were also recovered at Corbridge and are shown in the museum. The most famous of these is what has become known as the Corbridge Lion. This shows a marvellously detailed sculpture of a male lion pouncing on an unidentified prey species, like a cow-sized goat, and is the work of a master craftsman. It has been speculated that the carving was designed as a funerary piece to be placed upon a mausoleum, but was never used. The finding of the lion in what was the most obviously wealthy house in Corbridge shows that, at some point, the Romans reused the carving because its teeth have been removed and its mouth used as a water spout. This new use seems to have occurred in the third century and lasted only until the start of the next century. It would

Corstopitum (Agnethe CC BY 2.0 https://commons.wikimedia.org/wiki/File:Corstopitum_3.jpg)

seem that the lion had at some point become a symbol of the community at Corbridge as a more worn lion sculpture was recovered from a huge mausoleum called Shorden Brae. This unique tomb was built in the form of a tower and is one of the largest tombs to be known from the Roman Empire. The mausoleum was excavated in the 1950s and was measured 10 square metres, while the outer wall covered an area of 40 square metres. Obviously, this was the tomb of a wealthy and powerful person and it has been speculated that it may have been the monument to a legionary commander.

Opening Times
Check website: https://www.english-heritage.org.uk/visit/places/corbridge-
   roman-town-hadrians-wall/prices-and-opening-times/

Prices
Adult: £7.60
Child: £4.60
Concession: £6.80
Family (two Adults and up to three children): £19.80

Directions
Car – half a mile north-west of Corbridge on minor road then follow signs (sat-nav: NE45 5NT). Free parking for approximately twenty cars. Additional parking available in Corbridge, 1¼ miles distant.

Bus – 687 runs regularly from Hexham to Corbridge; 685 runs from Newcastle to Corbridge.

Train – Corbridge Station is approximately 1½ miles from the museum and there are regular services between Newcastle and Carlisle.

Facilities
Vending machine offering selection of hot drinks. Visitors are welcome to picnic in the grounds and there are benches. A shop sells a selection of English Heritage gifts and Roman-themed souvenirs. There are toilets and baby changing-facilities on site. Dogs on leads are welcome. An audio tour is included in the cost of entry and the site is family friendly.

Housesteads Roman Fort

Located approximately halfway along Hadrian's Wall, Housteads is the most complete example of a Roman fort in Britain. The fort was built at around the same time as the wall and housed an infantry regiment of 800 soldiers, known as a cohort. This is a large fort covering over 2 hectares and the fort hosted garrisons of auxiliaries from territories conquered by the Romans.

Excavations have shown that from the late second century to the fourth century the fort was garrisoned by the 1st Cohort of Tungrians. The Tungrians were a Germanic people from what is now Belgium and had previously been stationed on the wall at Vindolanda; a tomb slab from there identifies a Tungrian centurion as having lost his life between AD117–138. Further evidence of the Tungrians at Housesteads is given by a dedication to the gods and goddesses in accordance with the oracle of Apollo in Claros (now western Turkey). It is believed that this inscription might be connected with the outbreak of plague in AD 165.

Northern Granary at Housesteads (Frysland0109 CC BY-SA 3.0 https:// en.wikipedia.org/wiki/Housesteads_Roman_Fort#/media/File:Granary_at_ Housesteads_Roman_Fort.jpg)

Following Hadrian's death, his successor immediately advanced north and ordered the construction of the Antonine Wall in Scotland. Many historians believe that this led to the abandonment of Hadrian's Wall, but excavations have shown that there is no evidence of this at Housesteads as occupation seems to have been continuous. Certainly, some of the Tungrians manned defences on the new wall, but it seems that at least part of the cohort remained at Housesteads and it is believed that altars dedicated to Jupiter and Cocidius which were found here come from this period. The altars were dedicated by the soldiers of the 2nd Augustan Legion who were on garrison duty.

Once the Antonine Wall had been abandoned in AD 160, there were large-scale construction works undertaken at Housesteads and, during the early third century, there were a number of other garrison units housed here. These included soldiers from Frisia on the Rhine frontier (now north-east Holland) and seem to have included mercenaries.

By the end of the third century the civilian settlement which had formed outside the fort had contracted and largely vanished, and the size of the garrison at Housesteads was reduced. It is believed that many of the civilians from the outer settlement may have retreated within the walls of the fort for greater protection.

Opening Times
See website: https://www.english-heritage.org.uk/visit/places/housesteads-
    roman-fort-hadrians-wall/prices-and-opening-times/

Prices
Adults: £7.80
Children: £4.70
Concessionary: £7.00
Family (two Adults and up to three children): £20.30

Things to Do
Roman fort and tour.
Housesteads museum and Roman collection.
Visitor centre with extensive facilities.

Vindolanda

Just to the south of Hadrian's Wall lies the fort of Vindolanda. An auxiliary fort which was occupied from AD 85–370, Vindolanda guarded the important Stanegate Road and has provided some of the best Roman finds in the world. By the third century it is known that the garrison consisted of the 4th Cohort of Gauls. By this time the titles of the cohorts were largely nominal, but it appears that there was still a contingent of Gauls among the cohort as an inscription which was discovered reads: 'The troops from Gaul dedicate this statue to the goddess Gallia with the full support of the British-born troops.'

The site is privately owned, but offers a wonderful opportunity for visitors to experience life in a Roman fort.

The onsite museum is set in extensive gardens which contain a life-sized reconstruction of a Roman temple, shop, house and a more modern Northumbrian croft. The exhibits in the museum include footwear, armour, jewellery, and coins. The highlight of the collection, however, is the collection known as the Vindolanda Tablets. This collection of handwritten documents on wood are the second oldest surviving handwritten documents ever recovered in Britain and offer a unique glimpse into ordinary life on the frontier covering military and civilian matters.

Opening Times
Both Vindolanda and the Roman Army Museum are open daily from 9 February, 10 am – 5 pm.

Prices
Adult: £12.20
Child (5 – 17): £7.20
Senior/Student: £11.40
Family: £35.20

Further Details
Vindolanda offers the chance to take part in an archaeological dig too. There are also frequent display by the Roman Army re-enactors. See website for further details: http://www.vindolanda.com

Other Sites on the Wall

Chesters Roman Fort and Museum – the best-preserved Roman cavalry fort in Britain with a bath-house complex and museum of finds. (www.english-heritage.org.uk/visit/places/chesters-roman-fort-and-museum-hadrians-wall?

Walltown Crags – one of the best locations to walk a length of the wall as it stretches along the crags of the Whin Sill. (www.english-heritage.org.uk/visit/places/walltown-crags-hadrians-wall/)

CHAPTER 2

Anglo-Saxons

By AD 410 the Romans were gone. This left the north of England extremely vulnerable to attack. These attacks came from the Picts and Scots to the north, but historians also believe that the coastal areas were plagued by raiders from across the North Sea. These raiders were largely drawn from two main groups, the Angles from the border area of what is now Germany and Denmark, and the Saxons from present-day northern Germany.

These seaborne raiders had been a persistent problem in the final years of Roman rule, but as the Britons had been protected by the Roman army, the departure of the Romans left them largely defenceless. One solution was for communities of Romano-British to hire groups of these raiders as mercenaries who would defend them against their northern adversaries – and their own people from across the sea. This led to warbands of Anglo-Saxons being gifted with parcels of land in return for their service, but many of these Anglo-Saxons quickly realised that Britain was defenceless and ripe for occupation. There is great debate over how the Angles came to Northumberland (and indeed a wider debate on how the Anglo-Saxons came to Britain), whether primarily as invaders or as settlers. For many years the invasion theory held sway, but this has recently come under attack with more historians believing that the majority of Anglo-Saxons seem to have arrived as settlers, or protectors who then settled.

As we have seen, there was already a Teutonic presence in Northumberland. At Housesteads there were Teutonic soldiers and two of them raised a shrine which included dedications to their own deities. Teutonic garrisons, including Batavians, Frisians and Tungrians, occupied other sites including Carrawburgh and Vindobala (at Rudchester).

It is assumed that many of these auxiliaries remained behind when the Romans abandoned the British Isles. These men would often have married native women and would have raised families in the area, they would be settled, largely accepted, and unwilling to leave. Many of these Teutons would also be aware that, with the departure of the legions, the way was open for bands of their warriors to carve out their own territories by overthrowing native leaders.

Undoubtedly, there was extensive conflict during this period of approximately 200 years, but it may well have been mainly limited to fighting between an elite warrior- / ruling-class of rival warbands and minor chieftains. Evidence for actual happenings during the period are scant. In Northumberland there are rumours of a Celtic invasion from the north led by a leader named Cunedda and we do know that a Celtic kingdom named Bryneich was formed over much of what is now Northumberland. There is also, however, substantial evidence of Teutonic settlement. Place names are a good indicator of some of these early settlers and in Northumberland there are, for example, Chillingham, Bellingham, Eglingham, Edlingham, Ovingham Whittingham. Oddly, we can also detect some variation in regional or tribal dialects in these names. The first mentioned is pronounced as it is written while the others (and others further south from Chillingham) end phonetically in 'jum' (e.g. 'Whittinjum').

Upper Coquetdale seems to have been an especially popular area for early Teutonic settlements, with many of the names being of either Teutonic or Norse descent. The capital of Upper Coquetdale, Rothbury, comes from Hrotha's Burh – meaning Hrotha's fortified place.

This was the Age of Arthur and, like many areas of Britain, Northumberland has more than its fair share of stories claiming to be linked to that mythical king. Arthur was said to have fought twelve great battles before 516 and it is claimed the first of these was at the mouth of the River Glen, beside Wooler, while the tenth was fought at Trewhit in Upper Coquetdale where there is a large grave barrow. There are other legends which place Arthur holding court at Sewingshields on Hadrian's Wall and folklore says he and his court sleep there still, in some hidden place.

Returning to more sure ground, it was in approximately 547 that the Angle chief Ida the Flamebearer captured the coastal fort of Din Guyaroi (Bamburgh). It seems likely that Ida had already established a footing in what would become Northumberland by establishing bases in the Tyne valley. It was the seizing of Din Guyaroi, however, that was to prove pivotal in the establishment of his Kingdom of Bernicia. It would seem that Ida moved quickly and that in just three years he had successfully occupied much of not only Northumberland, but also the entire north east, including some territories in the south beside the River Tees in the Kingdom of Deira.

When Ida died in 560, he was the most powerful of the Anglian kings of the north, but his son Theoderic does not seem to have been as strong-willed as his father and was left only the Kingdom of Bernicia, north of the Tees. Many of the neighbouring Celtic kingdoms did not respect the rule of Theoderic and in 575 he found himself besieged at Bamburgh by Urien, the King of Rheged. Theoderic held out against this invasion, largely due to Urien being assassinated. It is impossible to be precise about where the siege took place, with accounts naming it as having occurred at either Bamburgh or the island of Lindisfarne (which may have been the first place that Ida conquered).

By 593, Bernicia was ruled over by King Aethelfrith. This king seems to have been cast more in the mould of his illustrious grandfather. Just five years into his reign he was said to have led his men to a great victory over the native Britons at Catterick. Despite this successful campaign it appears likely that large portions of the population remained Celtic Britons, although they were ruled over by Anglian lords.

Ten years later, King Aethelfrith took his forces north to face the Dalriadic Scottish King Aidan MacGabrain. The Scots had assembled a huge army and were assisted by a force from Ireland. Despite this, it was King Aethelfrith who emerged victorious and this victory enabled him to force the remaining Celtic kingdoms to acknowledge his power. It also allowed Aethelfrith to usurp the Kingdom of Deira and merge it with that of Bernicia in a kingdom named Northumbria. Many Deirans remained distrustful of Bernician rule and, although Aethelfirth attempted to settle them by marrying Acha, a member of the Deiran royal family, the main claimant to the throne of Deira, Acha's brother Edwin, fled to Mercia.

Aethelfrith remarried and it was in honour of his new wife, Bebba, that he renamed his royal seat (Bamburgh) Bebbanburgh. The main threat to Northumbria was now the southern Kingdom of Mercia and in 615, Aethelfrith successfully overthrew the King of Mercia, then later the same year won in battle against the Welsh and brought Cumbria into the Kingdom of Northumbria. Aethelfrith was now at the height of his power and he seemed destined for greatness. It was not to be; Aethelfrith was killed in battle the next year by King Raedwald of East Anglia (where Edwin had fled to).

The position in Northumbria was now reversed as Edwin, the Deiran, became king. The tensions between the two sub-kingdoms were still to the fore, however. Aethelfrith's son, Oswald, fled north where he was granted exile on the monastery isle of Iona, off the western Scottish coast. Edwin embarked on a series of conquests over minor Celtic holdout kingdoms in the south of his area of influence. Edwin also formed an alliance with the king of Kent, and in 625 he married Ethelberga, a princess from that kingdom. Edwin's growing power resulted in a botched assassination attempt by the king of the West Saxons in 626 (Edwin's son was born the same day), and this resulted in Edwin successfully defeating the West Saxons in battle and proclaiming himself Bretwalda (or High King of all England).

Like the kingdom she came from, Edwin's wife was a Christian and, following his victory over the West Saxons, Edwin attributed the victory to the Christian faith. In 627 Edwin took the decision to convert to Christianity himself and a process of conversion of many Northumbrians began. Paulinus, the new Bishop of York, is said to have baptised thousands of Northumbrians at sites such as the River Glen near Yeavering and at Holystone in Upper

Coquetdale. Rumours abound the site at Holystone, with some claiming that it was where King Edwin himself was baptised. This is not true, as it seems the king was baptised at York. It does, however, seem likely that Paulinus did indeed baptise a number of Northumbrian pagans at the site.

Lady's Well, Holystone - (Chris Gunns / Lady's Well, Holystone */ CC BY-SA 2.0)*

Edwin seems to have been particularly keen to not only enforce law and order upon his kingdom, but also to be seen to engage with the people frequently. He oversaw the construction of one of several royal palaces at Yeavering. The complex consisted of a great hall and a large wooden auditorium where audiences could be addressed by the king or other notables. It is also possible that the auditorium was used extensively for holding meetings of the royal court.

In 633 Edwin was slain in battle with the Mercians and the Welsh. Edwin's probable successor was also slain in the battle and Edwin's son, Edfrith, surrendered to King Penda of Mercia. The pagan Eanfrith, son of Aethelfrith, was crowned as the king of Bernicia but lasted only a year. His conqueror was King Cadwallon of Gynedd. King Oswald, however, returned from exile on Iona and slew King Cadwallon of Gwynedd at the Battle of Heavenfield.

Following the battle King Oswald installed an Irish monk named Aidan, whom he had met on Iona, with orders to oversee the conversion of Northumbria to Christianity. This was not the Roman version of Christianity however, but that of the Celtic Church. One of the features of this version of faith was its fascination with islands as places of solitude and reflection, and Aidan chose the island of Lindsifarne as the base for his bishopric, establishing a monastery on the island. Oswald oversaw the beginning of the re-Christianisation of Northumbria, but he remained a warrior king.

By 638 Oswald had captured Din Eidyn (Edinburgh) of the Gododdin (a Celtic speaking Brythonic people from the north-east, an area known as Hen Ogledd, the Old North – modern South-East Scotland and North-East England – who were descendants of the Votadini) and the Lothians became a part of Northumbria. Although Oswald oversaw the extension of his realm he was almost constantly at war and his southern border remained under threat from the growing power of Mercia under the rule of King Penda. So it was that in August of 642 Oswald was killed in battle with Penda, and the realm once again split in two with his brother Oswy succeeding in Bernicia, and Oswine, a Deiran noble who traced his ancestry, supposedly, back to the old Kings of Deira.

Oswine was beset on all sides; he lost ground to Penda and was then murdered shortly after he refused to meet a force under Oswy in battle.

Bolstered by this, Oswy reunited the kingdom but was faced with betrayal in Deira and an invasion led by Penda reached as far as Bamburgh before being repulsed. Determined to rid his kingdom of this threat, Oswy led his army against Penda in 655. Oswy was victorious; Penda and a large number of his followers were slain. Oswy then seized the northern parts of Mercia and was named as Bretwalda. Now secure in his power, Oswy was able to oversee cultural and religious developments in his vast kingdom.

Oswy died in 669 and was succeeded by his son Ecgfrith. Northumbria continued to expand under Ecgfrith's rule but in 673 he decided to divorce his chaste and virgin queen, Ethelreda, so that he could marry another. Under the influence of St Wilfrid of York, Ethelreda became a nun and was given a parcel of land around Hexham by her former husband. She immediately transferred ownership of this to Wilfrid and construction began on a monastery there. As a result of this there was growing tension between Ecgfrith and Wilfrid which culminated in the king banishing Wilfrid and breaking his diocese in two. The new bishopric of Hexham stretched from the River Tees to the River Tweed. Ecgfrith, determined not to be undermined by religious heads, ignored papal instructions which decried his splitting of the bishopric of York. Indeed, Ecgfrith went further and split the Hexham bishopric, hiving off a new bishopric of Lindisfarne which stretched from the Tweed to the River Aln.

Fresh from his victory over the religious authorities, Ecgfrith refused to listen to the advice of the former prior of Lindisfarne, Cuthbert, and in 684 launched an invasion of Meath in Ireland, but there was no lasting result from this attempted conquest. Cuthbert was at the time living as a hermit on Inner Farne, but he had already established a widespread reputation for healing the sick and for producing miracles. Ecgfrith, despite his refusal to listen to Cuthbert over the Meath invasion, came to respect and rely on the advice of the hermit and in 685 he arranged for Cuthbert to be appointed to the bishopric of Hexham; Cuthbert preferred Lindisfarne however, and was appointed as Bishop of Lindisfarne in 685.

Just one month after Cuthbert became bishop, King Ecgfrith was killed in battle against King Brude of Caledonia. The defeat was catastrophic in terms of any further attempt at Northumbrian expansion. Ecgfrith was succeeded by his illegitimate son, Aldfrith. The new king did not attempt to expand his kingdom militarily, but did oversee a period filled with the production of marvellous pieces of Celtic artwork.

In 686, St Cuthbert died on Inner Farne (he had resigned as bishop and returned to the life of a hermit earlier that year) and St Wilfrid returned to take over the bishopric, although he quickly transferred to Hexham. Wilfrid remained a contentious man and it took only four years for him to run into difficulties with the king once more. Again, it was over the right to create bishoprics and he was, once again, banished from Northumbria.

The latter part of the eighth century may have been a golden age for Northumbria scholarship (led by Bede of Jarrow), but it was also marked by continuing divisions between the two sub-kingdoms of Bernicia and Deira. When Aldfrith died in 705 he left his crown to his son, Osred, who, despite being a mere boy, managed to survive early threats due to the protection of Wilfrid, who returned to Hexham. Wilfrid died just four years later, but Osred managed to hold onto his crown despite an attempted invasion by the Picts. There was now a period of weak leadership and infighting beginning when Osred was murdered by his kinsmen, Cenred and Osric. The rule of Cenred lasted a very brief time and he was succeeded by Osric, who died in 729. He was in turn succeeded by the brother of Cenred, Ceolwulf. He made a poor king for an increasingly embattled kingdom as he was hugely pious and failed to gain the respect of his own subjects as a result. Over the next sixty-nine years, from 737, the kingdom of Northumbria was riven by internal fighting and had ten kings. Of these, five were expelled from their own kingdom, three were murdered (often by their own kin) and two gave up their crowns to become monks. During this period Northumbrian military might waned and its religious institutions collapsed into near-chaos. These crises were exacerbated by the Viking raids which began in 793 with an attack on Lindisfarne.

King Athelred does not seem to have been able to react to these raids in any effective manner and in 796 he was murdered at Corbridge. His murderer, Osbald, became king in his stead but lasted only a month. From 796–811 there were five different kings, none of whom could do anything to halt the decline of the kingdom. The last of these kings was Eanred, and although he lasted until 840, he could not stem the Viking raids on the east coast and Northumbria became a neglected and largely ignored isolated backwater.

The next king, Raedwulf, attempted to stem the raids but was killed by the Vikings in 844. In 865 both the church and monastery at Tynemouth were destroyed in a Viking raid and the nuns of St Hilda, who had gone there for safety, were massacred. By 866 Aelle was king of Northumbria, but the Norse raiders continued to be an escalating problem; towards the end of the year, an army of Vikings which had invaded Mercia turned their attention towards Northumbria and succeeded in sacking York. During the next year, King Aelle was killed attempting to take back York along with the Bernician noble, Earl Osbert. While the Vikings ruled over the southern part of what had been Northumbria, they appointed a puppet king named Egbert. In 870 Tynemouth Priory was again plundered by the Vikings and in 872 the Bernician nobility rejected the rule of Egbert.

The year 875 was a catastrophic one for those who lived in what was to become Northumberland. The monks of Lindisfarne, with the coffin of St Cuthbert, had already been forced from the island by Viking raids, and after a period at Norham were forced from this sanctuary too. The Vikings then attacked on the River Tyne, again sacking Tynemouth Priory and mounting a winter campaign during which they also sacked Hexham. Most of what became Northumberland, while beaten militarily, was not occupied by the Vikings except for certain pockets of land, but the great kingdom was no more.

Northumberland was now an earldom, but had been greatly weakened. Earl Eadwulf died in 913, and in the next year an army of Irish-Norwegian Vikings attacked Corbridge but were beaten by a combined force of Northumbrians and Scots. They returned the next year and defeated a combined Northumbrian, Dane and Frankish army at Corbridge. Once again, however, the majority of these Vikings did not settle in what was now Northumberland and instead settled in County Durham.

Battle of Heavenfield

Following the death of King Edwin of Northumbria, his enemy, King Cadwallon of Gwynedd, invaded the northern kingdom. He was met in battle at Heavenfield, to the east of Chollerford, by King Oswald. Having returned from exile on Iona, King Oswald quickly raised an army (including some Scots) and, though outnumbered, took up a defensive position to face Cadwallon. He chose the site wisely; knowing that he was outnumbered, he planned to force the Welsh king to engage on a narrow front. The night before the battle King Oswald claimed to have seen a vision of St Columba in which he was promised victory, urging him, in the words of God to Joshua, to 'Be strong and of good courage, I will be with you.' That morning, Oswald had a huge cross erected and prayed before it with his army.

According to Oswald's intentions, the battle itself saw the Welsh attack on a narrow front, being hemmed in by terrain and by the remains of Hadrian's Wall. The Welsh were unable to use their greater numbers and were routed by the combined Northumbria and Scots force with many being cut down as they fled. King Cadwallon himself was caught and killed at a site named as the Brook of Denis, which is assumed to be the Rowley Burn. Of an estimated 1,000-strong Welsh force,

The Cross at Heavenfield (© drhfoto/Adobe Stock)

it is believed that 80 per cent were slain. In gratitude for his victory, the site became known as Heavenfield and a church was erected on the battlefield.

This is the account as given largely by the Venerable Bede who was writing some 100 years after events, although he had access to a contemporary account written by an Ionian abbot. However, Bede, as always, has placed his own interpretation on events. It would seem that rather than divine intervention, the battle was won largely by the inspired leadership and tactical ability of the young King Oswald. In his choice of battlefield he forced the Welsh to charge uphill on a narrow front and gave his own men every advantage. His own force was placed between two escarpments on their flanks, and had Hadrian's Wall to their south. The account of Cadwallon's death is also based largely on hearsay and it is equally likely that Cadwallon was cut down on the main battlefield. Likewise, Bede's glorying of the battle as a victory of Christianity over Paganism is false. Although it is true that Oswald was a particularly pious king for this era, it is likely that some of the men who fought on his side were pagans while Cadwallon had himself been baptised and some of his force would have been followers of his faith.

St Oswald's church is also well worth a visit, even though most of the visible portions date to only the Victorian period. The original Saxon church that was placed where the forces of King Oswald were arrayed was rebuilt by the Normans, and then rebuilt yet again in the eighteenth century and modified by the Victorians. The church still seems to have an air of antiquity and unusually has no electricity, being lit only by gas lamps and candles.

Directions

Car – follow the B6318 along the line of Hadrian's Wall and the cross marking the battle site is clearly visible a mile east of Chollerford. There is a layby for cars at the site and the church, which is easily accessible via a short path, contains an interesting account of the battle.

Foot – Heavenfield lies on the St Oswald's Way pilgrimage route which runs from Heavenfield to Lindisfarne and on the very popular Hadrian's Wall path long distance trail.

Lindisfarne Priory

Built in 635, the priory at Lindisfarne was founded by St Aidan, an Irish monk who was brought from Iona by King Oswald. It went on to become one of the most important centres of early English Christianity, the centre of the cult of St Cuthbert and the site of the creation of the beautiful Lindisfarne Gospels. Aidan was highly successful in his mission to bring Celtic Christianity to Northumbria, and from his seat on Lindisfarne, oversaw the establishment of the faith and of several monasteries and other religious houses in the kingdom.

In the 670s a monk named Cuthbert joined the monastery after seeing a vision while herding livestock. After becoming Prior of Lindisfarne, Cuthbert oversaw the conversion of the monastery to Roman Christianity; as a result he was viewed with some distrust and anger by some of the monks, which led him to resign and live as a hermit on a small island just offshore, named St Cuthbert's Isle after him, and then on the far more remote island of Inner Farne. Cuthbert remained popular with the reigning nobles, and in 685 he was convinced by the king to end his period of solitude and to accept the bishopric of Lindisfarne. Over the next couple of years he enjoyed a fine reputation as a seer, healer and man of faith, with extensive influence over kings, the faith in England, and with strong links to the continent, including with the empire of Charlemagne.

When Cuthbert died in March 687, he was buried in the church at Lindisfarne in a stone coffin. When this coffin was reopened by the monks in 698 they found that his corpse had not decayed at all. This news quickly spread and was widely seen as a sign of Cuthbert's purity and saintliness. His remains were placed in a raised coffin-shrine and, as a series of miracles were reported, a cult of St Cuthbert began to form.

With the cult firmly established, the monastery became a popular place of pilgrimage and attracted grants of land and money from kings and nobles, becoming wealthy and influential. This also meant that it attracted more monks and Lindisfarne quickly became a site of Christian learning with the remarkable Lindisfarne Gospels being produced there in the early eighth century.

This all came to a calamitous end in June 793 when the Vikings made their first significant attack on Britain (and indeed Western Europe).

The target was none other than the rich, but vulnerable, island monastery of Lindisfarne. Alcuin, a British scholar working for the Frankish King Charlemagne, wrote, in a source now lost, of how the raiders had desecrated this most holy site, had slain monks at the altar of St Cuthbert, and had 'trampled the remains like dung in the street'. The raid caused widespread horror among the English church because St Cuthbert had not intervened to prevent the destruction and slaughter. While Alcuin was appalled at the slaughter, he also proposed a possible reason for the saint's failure to protect the community. Just weeks before the raid a nobleman named Sicga had been buried there. Sicga had apparently led a conspiracy which resulted in the murder of King Aelfwald of Northumbria in 788, but in 793 he was reported to have killed himself. Alcuin asked the Bishop of Lindisfarne if the burial of a known suicide who was guilty of regicide had led to the raid. The bishop ignored the question, seeing it, probably correctly, as another example of Alcuin attempting to cause mischief and sow discord.

More minor raids followed and by the 830s the monks of Lindisfarne had largely abandoned their island and retreated to Northam. The monks

Lindisfarne Church (© David Rice/Adobe Stock)

alternated between the two sites for the next forty-five years before deciding in 875 to abandon Lindisfarne for good. For the next seven years the monkish community wandered the north east, carrying with them the remains of St Cuthbert in his coffin, along with the remaining treasure of Lindisfarne. They eventually settled in County Durham, where St Cuthbert's remains are still.

Someone remained at Lindisfarne, however, as more than fifty intricately carved stones used as Christian grave markers have been found and dated to the period between the late eighth century and the early tenth century. Many of these carvings are found in the museum on site. Perhaps the most remarkable grave marker is the one which is known as the 'Viking Domesday stone', and clearly shows armed men brandishing swords and axes of the Viking style. This remarkable stone features a depiction of Domesday on the reverse side. The grave markers were probably buried underground so as to protect them from further raiders and this has resulted in them being better preserved than they otherwise would have been. Some of the markers also feature the name of the man or woman buried with it. These names are carved in either capital letters or in runes.

In 1069 the monks of Durham fled with the remains of their beloved saint in order to escape the Norman harrying of the north. So St Cuthbert returned, briefly, to Lindisfarne. After the monks had returned to Durham they decided to establish an outpost on Lindisfarne in order to restore their link to the holy site and to establish their rights to be seen as the guardians of St Cuthbert and his legacy. It is not known when exactly this community was formed, but it is known that a monk from Durham named Edward was living there by 1122 and there are references to a full community being resident fifty years later.

The church, the remains of which can be seen now, was built in the 1150s and included a cenotaph on the site of the tomb of St Cuthbert. The numbers of the community remained small, peaking at around ten in the thirteenth century, and it became traditional for monks from Durham to stay at Lindisfarne for a few years before they returned to their own house.

After Edward I invaded Scotland, the Borders became a place of warfare and, despite their warm relationship with the Scottish crown through the twelfth century, the monks of Lindisfarne feared for their lives during

Lindsifarne Church, clearly showing the Rainbow Arch (© Hans Peter Denecke/ Adobe Stock)

the long period of Scottish raiding following Bannockburn and had the priory fortified. In 1385, however, the monks petitioned King Richard II for permission to dismantle the fortifications, claiming they could no longer afford to pay for the garrison that was required. Despite the strife on the border Lindisfarne appears to have gotten off relatively unscathed and there is evidence that the monks there lived in increasing luxury. A number of the fortifications can still be seen, including a very rare example of a defended monastery gateway.

The priory was closed with the dissolution of the monasteries and the Reformation in the early sixteenth century, but thankfully the buildings were not dismantled. In fact, it appears that Lindisfarne played some part in the vision for the defence of the realm because three earth and timber defensive fortifications were erected around the harbour. At the east end of the Heugh lies a rare surviving example of a small sixteenth century fort which has survived without significant alteration. There were also extensive plans for further defences around the entire island but these never advanced beyond the planning stages.

By the late eighteenth century the picturesque remains were attracting both tourists and artists; it appears that the church was largely intact at this period, but at some point before the 1820s the central tower and south aisle had collapsed. The site was purchased by a Mr Selby, but despite his attempts to care for the remains, the west front collapsed at some point in the 1850s. In the late nineteenth century the site was still attracting tourists and pilgrims; the monastic buildings were excavated by Sir William Crossman and a few years later, in the early twentieth century, the church area was also excavated and the walls strengthened and consolidated against further erosion. Further archaeological exploration was undertaken in the 1980s and this revealed a ninth-century farmstead on the north of the island at Greenshiel. This exploration uncovered hundreds of bones from young cattle at the farmstead and it has been suggested that this might have been a site used for the preparation of the large amounts of parchment that were used in the monastery's scriptorium.

Directions

Car – turn off the A1 for Beal (14 miles south of Berwick-upon-Tweed). From Beal follow the signs for Holy Island (the other name for Lindisfarne), a distance of approximately 5 miles (Sat-Nav: TD15 2RX).

Note that Holy Island is accessed by a tidal causeway which is submerged rapidly at high tide. Please only attempt to access the island at the approved times which are posted at the causeway entrance and are available online at https://www.holy-island.info/lindisfarnecastle/2019/.

Rail – the nearest station is Berwick-upon-Tweed

Bus – Arriva service X18 runs to Beal from Newcastle and Berwick three times a day. Arriva service X15 runs seven times a day (Monday – Saturday) from Newcastle and Berwick. Borders Bus service 477 runs a regular (Monday – Saturday) between Berwick station and Holy Island, for timetables see https://www.bordersbuses.co.uk/images/timetables-2018/477-online-2019.pdf

Pricing

Adult: £6.80

Child (5 – 17): £4.10

Concession: £6.10

Family (two adults, up to three children): £17.70

Facilities

A pay and display car park is sited five minutes walk from the site.

Visitors are welcome to picnic on the grass although there are no tables.

There is a large shop on site which stocks a wide range of English Heritage products as well as a range of wines and preserves with regular tasting sessions.

The nearest toilets are in the village.

Dogs on leads are welcome in the Priory but not in the shop/museum.

The museum charts the history of Lindisfarne and includes many items of interest from the site.

Pushchairs are allowed on site.

For those wishing to stay on this beautiful island there is the Coastguards Cottage. This three-bedroom cottage sleeps six plus a cot and is in the village only a short walk from the Priory. The cottage has been extensively converted for use by those with mobility issues. For availability and prices check: https://www.english-heritage.org.uk/visit/holiday-cottages/find-a-holiday-cottage/Coastguards-Cottage-Lindisfarne-Priory/availability-and-prices/

Bamburgh Castle

Occupying 9 acres of a rocky plateau which rises above the beautiful Northumbrian coastline, Bamburgh is a fascinating site. Archaeological evidence has suggested that people occupied the site for a very long period. Mesolithic flint spear-tips have been recovered and there have been Bronze

Age burials recorded here. The Romans, ever keen to take advantage of a naturally defensive position, also occupied the site which they named Din Guayrdi. A timber camp was built by them and was occupied by both Roman troops and Votadini collaborators. It seems, however, that the Votadini did not occupy the site after the Romans left and burned the camp down.

The first written records of Bamburgh hint at it being the first place that the Angles landed in Northumbria, and that it was first occupied by a warrior lord named Ida who built a timber hall house on the rock and placed a hedge around it. The hedge was later replaced by a stone wall and Ida and his descendants quickly expanded their kingdom of Bernicia so that it came to comprise the entirety of the north from the River Humber to the Forth. This marked the beginning of Bamburgh's greatest and most glamourous period. It was Ida's grandson, King Ethelfrith, who changed the name of the site. He chose the name Bebbanburg (or fortified town on the isolated rock) and expanded the nascent settlement.

Between 617–670, the successive Anglian Kings Edwin, Oswald and Oswiu were acknowledged as Bretwaldas, or High Kings of England, and Bamburgh, as their capital, became a place of very great importance. Indeed, it could be said that for this brief time Bamburgh was the capital of England. When Oswiu died in February 670 it marked a decrease in Northumbrian power and by 828 the kings of Northumbria were vassals of the kings of Wessex. By 954 the long line of Anglian descendants of Ida's line had ended and the first Earl of Northumberland, Oswulf, was in possession of Bamburgh. In the eleventh century the Vikings sacked Bamburgh and when the Normans conquered England the fortifications and city were in a pitiable state.

Like the Romans, the Normans also had a keen eye for a defensible site and work began to repair and strengthen Bamburgh. However, it was not until the reign of King Henry I that work was started on the keep. The keep is a massive structure and took a long time to build; finally being completed during the reign of Stephen, it received its first attack in 1138 when King David I of Scotland launched his invasion of Northumberland. After this the castle (along with Newcastle) was one of the only places to be exempt from the Scottish earldom of Northumberland.

From 1216–72 there was significant growth at Bamburgh as a grange consisting of a large hall house, and it is speculated that the current King's Hall is a modern recreation of the chamber. Among the substantial improvements made at this time was the creation of a port at Warenmouth. This was seen as necessary as trade was increasing at Bamburgh.

During the reign of King Edward II, Bamburgh was used as a prison/house for the king's favourite, Piers de Gaveston, when the barons grew increasingly irked by his presence. Gaveston had retreated to Bamburgh following his utter failure as Constable of Scotland, but was held under informal house-arrest on the authorities of the barons. He was allowed some freedom, but on 3 November 1311, Gaveston was banished from the kingdom. After Edward's defeat at Bannockburn in 1314, the king fled to Bamburgh by boat on his way south. Bamburgh suffered along with the rest of Northumberland in the years following Bannockburn, not helped by the fact that the constable of Bamburgh Castle, Robert de Horsley, refused to allow the townspeople to purchase a truce costing £270 with Robert the Bruce unless they paid him a similar sum. This meant that the people could not afford the truce and were raided. This was not the only nefarious action of de Horsley, as it was also claimed that he allowed his porter to charge exorbitant rates for entering and leaving the castle and that he seized cargoes from ships at Warenford. Because of the long list of complaints against him, he was removed from his position in 1316.

Upon becoming king, Edward III immediately appointed a Robert de Horncliffe as constable and he made a thorough report on the state of the castle. This saw substantial repairs made and once again Bamburgh was restored to a suitable condition for a royal castle. During his campaign against the Scots, Edward lodged his wife, Philippa of Hainault, in Bamburgh before his defeat of the Scots at the Battle of Halidon Hill. These repairs rendered the castle practically impregnable, but for the townspeople below it was a different story and an unsuccessful attempt was made to raise funds for a town wall.

The Wars of the Roses, 1455–1485, proved tragic for Bamburgh. In 1463 a 10,000-strong Yorkist force under the Earl of Warwick besieged the 300 defenders of Bamburgh and forced the garrison to capitulate due to lack of food. The following spring the castle was retaken by a combined Scottish and French force acting on behalf of the Lancastrians. The Lancastrians held the castle for the next nine months with King Henry ruling from Bamburgh. After the Lancastrians suffered the reverses at Hedgely Moor and at Hexham in 1464, Henry was forced to flee to Bamburgh but did not remain there long, leaving Sir Ralph Grey in charge. Thus, it fell to Sir Ralph to attempt to hold out against the forces of the Earl of Warwick when he laid siege to Bamburgh in 1464. Sir Ralph refused terms of surrender and King Edward IV, Henry was also calling himself king at the time, ordered two of his guns, believed to be named 'Newcastle' and 'London', to be brought up and used against the castle. The castle walls had not been designed to hold out against such force and the guns quickly blew holes into the fortress. Realising his position was hopeless, Sir Ralph quickly ordered the surrender of the castle. Bamburgh thus found itself occupying a place in the history books as it became the first English castle to be brought low by the new technology of gunfire. In 1465 Henry was captured and imprisoned in the Tower of London. He was released and came back to claim the throne once more in 1470 but reigned for only six months until Edward IV returned with Burgundian assistance. Henry was captured once more, and his son killed at the Battle of Tewkesbury. Henry was likely murdered while in the Tower on 21 May 1471.

At some point during the reign of Queen Elizabeth I, Bamburgh was awarded to Lord Warden of the Marches, Sir John Forster. The warden was an old and wily border ruffian who was heavily involved in much of the reiving which affected the borders during the period. Sir John had another home at Adderstone, but he spent the final years of his extremely long life at Bamburgh, dying there in 1602 at the remarkable age of 102.

The castle passed down through Forster's descendants, but they proved to be a disreputable lot and squandered the family's money. By 1704, the then owner, another Sir John Forster, was forced to sell his estates in order to settle his debts. His estates were bought by his son-in-law, Nathaniel Crew, Bishop of Durham. When Lord Crew died in 1721 he left his estates to a charitable trust and it was one of the trustees, Dr John Sharp, who oversaw the next great endeavour at Bamburgh.

Among the things which Dr Sharp accomplished was the establishment of a free school for the children of the village (provided their parents earned less than £60 per year), a coastguard service which expanded to include a lifeboat, beacon, and rescue equipment – rescued seamen were allowed to be housed at the castle free of charge for a week. Dr Sharp also enacted a scheme which allowed him to purchase corn for the poor inhabitants, and then developed a shop which provided necessary supplies to the poor of the parish. This indomitable and visionary man then oversaw the establishment of a chemists' shop, a surgery, an infirmary with a maternity wing to look after the health of the poor of the parish.

After Dr Sharp died in 1792, many of the services continued for some time, but they then began to fail as local authorities took on more responsibility and the poor management of the remaining trustees led to a decline in funds. By 1863 there was an inquiry into the charity which found that trustees were living at Bamburgh rent free, while the funds of the trust were in an atrocious state. This resulted in the closure of the school and by the early 1890s the remaining charities set up by Dr Sharp were forced to close.

In 1894 Bamburgh Castle changed hands once more when the industrialist and genius Lord Armstrong of Cragside bought the property for the sum of £60,000. He had finished his long work at his Cragside home and had visions of creating a gothic castle at Bamburgh. As a result he spent £1,000,000 on the building and placed modern conveniences such as electricity and even central heating in the ancient castle. His modifications did not found universal favour, however, with some saying he had spoilt the historic nature of the castle. This is a harsh judgement and it should be recognised that although much of the remains at Bamburgh are indeed somewhat more modern than expected, there are also substantial Norman remains. The great keep, gatehouse, towers and some other parts are clearly Norman and provide great interest to the historian.

Directions

Car – take B1342 turning at Belford, Bamburgh is clearly signposted. Parking is available at £2 and gives access not only to the castle but also to the village and beach (Sat-Nav NE69 7DF). Map reference: NU184 351.

Bus – regular services are available. Arriva service X18 goes to Bamburgh from Newcastle via Morpeth, Warkworth and Alnwick.

Rail – train to either Berwick-upon-Tweed or Alnmouth and then a bus to Bamburgh.

Opening Times
February – November (check website for details). Last admission 4 pm.

Admission Prices
Adult: £10.95
Child: £5
Under 5s: Free
Family Ticket (two adults and up to three dependents): £26

Visitor Information
Prams and pushchairs are welcome in the grounds but must be left at the entrance to the state rooms. There is internal storage provided and Hippychicks (baby and toddler hip carriers) are available for parents to borrow. Only registered guide dogs are allowed on the site.

Maelmin

While experiencing the wonders of Yeavering Bell it is well worth the very short detour to the village of Milfield to experience the remains of a royal township from the days of Anglian dominance. Maelmin was the site of one of the royal households of the kings of Northumbria, and as such was once one of the most important places in Anglo-Saxon Britain. Today it is home to a number of reconstructions of local archaeological discoveries.

These reconstructions are not solely limited to the Anglo-Saxon age and include a reconstruction of one of the many henges, dating from around 2,000 BC, which were found in the area. The henge has its entrance aligned to the culturally and spiritually important Cheviot Hills, and it was probably a cult centre where people prayed and celebrated. At least eight henges in the Till Valley formed a processional way, and the reconstruction is based on the Milfield North Henge which was located in a field near the current reconstruction site. Almost 3,000 years after its creation, the henge was used as a burial place by the Anglo-Saxons.

Excavations which took place at the nearby quarry revealed the remains of a number of settlements which dated from 4,000 BC – 570 AD. Among the finds were three rectangular wooden houses dating from the Dark Ages. It is believed that these houses were part of a small farming community.

Above left: *Entrance Stone at Maelmin (tormentor4555 CC BY-SA 3.0 https:// commons.wikimedia.org/wiki/File:Maelmim_entrance_stone_-_panoramio.jpg)*

Above right: *Reconstruction of Henge at Maelmin ((Lisa Jarvis /* Maelmin - reconstruction of henge */ CC BY-SA 2.0 https://commons.wikimedia.org/wiki/ File:Maelmin_-_reconstruction_of_henge_-_geograph.org.uk_-_420808.jpg)*

Unfortunately, it has not been determined whether the houses belonged to native Britons or Anglian newcomers. The visitor to Maelmin can visit an accurate reconstruction of the largest of these Dark Age houses, measuring some 7 x 3.25 metres.

Milfield became important once more in the 1940s when RAF Milfield was constructed. Lying in the fields to the south of the henge reconstruction, RAF Milfield became home to the Fighter Leaders' School and one of the primary locations for training RAF and US pilots in ground-attack techniques in the build-up to the D-Day Landings.

Prices

Maelmin is free to visit but it is requested that dogs be kept on a lead, especially during lambing season, and visitors are welcome to make a voluntary donation (https://www.maelmin.org.uk)

CHAPTER 3

Medieval Northumberland

Throughout the long Medieval period Northumberland found itself on the front-lines of the Anglo-Scottish Wars, and this led to massive devastation in the county with thousands being killed or forced to flee from the ferocity of Scottish raiding and invasion, while passing English armies also made excessive demands on the county. The constant state of warfare and tension also resulted in a huge programme of fortification which resulted in Northumberland having more castles and towers than any other county in Britain. In addition to the castles which are included in detail here, there are a wide variety of medieval ruins and remains that can easily be found online by the interested visitor.

In the wake of the Scottish succession crisis following the death of both King Alexander III and his young daughter, 1286–1290, King Edward I was approached to arbitrate on the question as to who would inherit the crown of Scotland. This placed him in a tricky position as the kings of England had long claimed overlordship of the northern realm and Edward himself had a claim through his descent from King Malcolm III. In 1292 he chose John Balliol, Lord of Bywell in Northumberland and Barnard Castle in County Durham. In truth, Balliol probably did have the strongest claim, but it is possible that Edward chose him because he saw him as more malleable than the other contenders (primarily the Bruce family).

After becoming king, however, Balliol, despite the fact that he had done homage to Edward at Newcastle on 26 December 1292, seems to have believed that he was equal in power to both his predecessors and to King Edward. Relations between the two men and the two realms deteriorated quickly and in 1294 when, supported by his nobles, King John refused to send Scottish barons to take part in Edward's war with France, the matter came to a head. A year later Scotland formed an alliance with France and a furious Edward declared King John a traitor. In 1296 Edward mounted a brief, yet brutal, campaign which subjugated Scotland and saw Berwick being taken and sacked. King John was humiliated and removed as king before being exiled, and English garrisons manned Scottish towns and castles.

Resistance in Scotland was sporadic but violent, with Sir William Wallace and Andrew Moray leading an early revolt which included a brutal raid into Northumberland in 1296; it was when Robert the Bruce rebelled against Edward in 1306, following his murder of rival John Comyn of Badenoch, however, that the war really reignited.

Against all odds, Robert the Bruce was wildly successful in putting down his Scottish opponents, rallying the people of Scotland, and then retaking English garrisons. It was made possible partially by the weaknesses of the new English king, Edward II, who had taken over following his father's death in July 1307. The success of Bruce culminated in the defeat of Edward II and his army at Bannockburn in 1314, and this paved the way for a long period (1314–28) during which Northumberland was harrowed by successive Scottish invasions and raids.

King Robert's intentions during these raids was not in conquest, but in securing much-needed funds to replenish his depleted treasury. While he largely ignored the castles and their garrisons, the poorer folk of Northumberland were not so lucky and large tracts of the county were left utterly devastated and, in places, unpopulated as people fled south from the Scottish threat. For example, the south Tweedside estates belonging to the monks of Durham, and including the churches of Norham and Holy Island, were left so devastated that income had declined from £280 (£200,700 today) in 1314–15 to just £23 (£16,990) in 1320–21; at one point, income for 1318–19 was just £9 (or £5,803 today). The story was the same across much of Northumberland and many communities were annihilated or left in penury by a government which seemed to have abandoned them. Many communities, especially further south, bought Bruce off by offering to pay blackmail to him in order to escape Scottish depredations.

Even communities in southern Northumberland, however, were certainly not exempt from Scottish predation. Ponteland, for example, declined in value from a peacetime valuation of £34 5s 11d to just £4 0s 2d by 1325, and at Ingoe, near Stamfordham, a similar situation prevailed, while none of the tenant holdings were let because they had all been destroyed by Scots raids. Across the county, landlords' incomes fell by an average of 80 per cent.

Many of the Northumbrian nobility were also left with crippling debts to be paid to the Scots as a result of having to ransom family members who had been taken prisoner in the fighting. Many Northumbrians were captured at Bannockburn and in the subsequent invasions and raids. The situation of many Northumbrian nobles was not helped by the unwillingness of the crown to reimburse them for the expenses they had incurred in its service. The Lord of Ellingham, Robert Clifford, for example requested an annual pension of £62 per annum, claiming that during the war he had been compelled to pay £100 in ransom following his capture at Bannockburn, had lost horses and armour to the value of over £66, and had served in the Berwick garrison at his own expense during a six-year period in which his estates income had declined by £100.

In such a bleak situation it was perhaps inevitable that some of the Northumbrian nobility, feeling abandoned by the crown, took matters into their own hands and turned to brigandage. The most famed of these Northumbrian brigands was the Mitford Gang. Led in the field by Sir Gilbert de Middleton of Cramlington, and Hartley and Sir Walter Selby of Seghill, the gang included many of the minor nobility and led a series of raids upon their neighbours and levied blackmail on quite a large scale. The gang was undoubtedly the pawn of Sir John de Eure (who owned land at Kirkley), who commanded the garrison at Mitford Castle (the garrison appears to have formed some of the muscle behind the gang) and, through him, Thomas, Earl of Lancaster, a scheming man who aimed to overthrow King Edward II.

The gang quickly established a very effective operation in which they approached landowners who still had land in cultivation and demanded that they join the gang. If they were met with refusal or resistance, the gang quickly took violent action, wasting crops and stealing livestock and goods. By 1317 almost eighty Northumberland landowners were involved in the gang. By now the gang was extremely confident and was extending its operations into County Durham. Demonstrating how far the enforcement of law had fallen the gang undertook its most audacious operation in August 1317.

Learning that the newly elected Bishop of Durham, Lewis de Beaumont, was to make his way to Durham for his enthronement, accompanied only by a small party including his brother Henry, Middleton and Selby quickly gathered a small party together and mounted an ambush at Rushyford. They quickly subdued the clerical party and carried off both the bishop and his brother into Northumberland where they were imprisoned in Mitford Castle to be ransomed at a future date. Among the bishop's group were two cardinals, Gaucelin D'Eauze and Luca Fieschi, sent as papal envoys to discuss peace proposals with King Robert. The two cardinals were not taken, but they were robbed of all their goods.

This bold move was a step too far, and what was left of the authorities and loyal nobility in Northumberland rose against the gang. By early December, Middleton and his brother, John, had been captured when Mitford fell to Sir William de Felton. The two were taken to London, tried, and hanged, drawn and quartered as traitors on 26 January 1318. Selby, however, who seems to have been a wily fighter and skilled ruffian, escaped capture and continued with his depredations from Horton Tower, near Blyth. Typically, he had seized the tower from near neighbour, Sir Bertram Monboucher. Seeing the writing on the wall Selby fled to Scotland where he was welcomed. When the Scots took Mitford Castle in 1318, King Robert placed Selby in command of it. He lived here in a state of near-siege until 1321 when he surrendered. He spent the next six years languishing in the Tower of London before being released. Selby continued his adventurous life by taking part, usually on the English side, in the wars between England and Scotland, before he was captured by the Scottish King David in 1346. He was forced to watch the execution of his two eldest sons before he was himself executed.

As we have seen, Northumberland had been left partly devastated by 1327. Bruce invaded once more in this year. King Edward II had been overthrown by his queen and her lover, Roger Mortimer, who placed the 14-year-old Edward III on the throne, and Bruce, aware of his own weakening condition, decided to take advantage of the situation. His own raid was followed by others led by two of his lieutenants, and this time the crown took some responsibility and an English army moved north, only to fail to bring the wily Scots to battle. This final exertion by the English bankrupted the exchequer and resulted in the English suing for peace. The Treaty of Northampton was signed in May 1328 and Northumberland could breath easier. The county seems to have recovered well. The south Tweedside records of the monks of Durham show that estate incomes increased from just £22 in 1327–28 to £220 by 1330–31.

The peace between the two nations was not to last. King Edward III chafed under the control of his mother and Mortimer, overthrwing them in 1330. He proved himself a forceful king and was no doubt aided by the fact that King Robert I, who had died in 1329, was succeeded by the infant King David II. Edward decided almost immediately to undo the Treaty of Northampton and support a group of lords who had been disinherited by Robert the Bruce along with Edward Balliol, the son of King John Balliol. Among this group, known as the 'disinherited', were two Northumbrians, Gilbert de Umfraville and David of Strathbogie. The two men, despite being Northumbrians, claimed the earldoms of Angus and Atholl respectively.

By 1333 Balliol had Berwick under siege and the town need urgent relief. The Scots, under Sir Archibald Douglas, responded by invading Northumberland and threatening Bamburgh where King Edward's queen was residing. Edward ignored this and instead ordered the hanging of one of the Scottish hostages taken from Berwick. The English forced the Scots into a similar position which had pertained at Bannockburn. The Scots were forced to attempt a relief of Berwick with the two forces meeting on 19 July at Halidon Hill, at the far tip of Northumberland, just across the border from Scotland today. The Scottish army was utterly routed and Berwick capitulated the very next day. It appeared that Edward Balliol would be successful, but by 1341 the English forces in Scotland had once again been defeated.

King David II proved to be aggressive and, once again, Northumberland found itself on the front-lines as he led a raid as far as the Tyne in 1342. In 1346, at the request of the French, he invaded England through Cumbria and led his army down the Tyne valley to devastate Hexham. This invasion culminated with the Scots being defeated at the Battle of Neville's Cross and David II being taken prisoner.

This changed the situation completely for Northumberland, and from 1347 there was relative peace for the next thirty years (although Berwick was captured by the Scots and then retaken in 1355–56). For many Northumbrians this was a breathing space where life could return to normal; the county quickly recovered and rebuilt from the losses it had suffered. However, although the war had seemingly ended, Northumberland (and other northern counties) had also fallen victim to a natural disaster during the period of warfare. It was not only the Scottish raids which devastated the county, but successive appalling summers in 1315–17 resulted in extremely poor harvests and were followed by an epidemic of disease which decimated livestock. It is now believed that this natural disaster led to a fall in population nationally of over 15 per cent – greater in Northumberland. So severe was the collapse in Northumberland that no figures have survived and historians continue to debate just how severe the fall was in the county.

As the fourteenth century progressed there were significant changes beginning to affect Northumbrian society. One of the most significant for the landowning classes was the disappearance of the many cross-border estates which had been commonplace before the wars of independence. This affected both large and small landowners. The lordship of Tynedale, for example, had traditionally been held by the Scottish king, but this was confiscated and passed through a number of different hands until it was finally acquired by Queen Philippa (King Edward III's wife) after it had become a crown possession in 1336.

The putting down of the Mitford Gang also resulted in substantial changes to land ownership in Northumberland. The estate of John Middleton, which included the manor of Belsay, for example, was granted to John de Strivelyn as recompense for the heavy ransom he had paid to secure his release from Scottish captivity.

Edward III died in 1377 and was succeeded by the 10-year-old Richard II. The presence of a child-monarch, the constant scheming of the ambitious John of Gaunt and the challenge of the Peasants' Revolt of 1381 in England led to increased instability and the renewal of the war in 1384, when the Scots once more launched a series of raids into Northumberland and Cumbria. One of these raids reached as far as Tynemouth and returned with prisoners and booty. When the Scots launched their main offensive, it came in the west and the attack into Northumberland, led by the earls of Douglas and March, was a diversionary manoeuvre.

Douglas led his force as far south as Newcastle, where the Scots skirmished but refused to directly attack as the walls were too strong. During this skirmishing Douglas unhorsed the English knight Sir Henry 'Hotspur' Percy and took his pennon as a trophy. Hotspur, named for his impetuosity and temper, was the son and heir of the 1st Earl of Northumberland and was commander of Newcastle. He pursued and caught up with Douglas near Otterburn and in a fierce and confused night-time battle Douglas was killed, but Hotspur and numerous others taken prisoner. The Battle of Otterburn was seen and reported widely as a Scottish victory and provided the main success of this Scottish invasion.

With a peace treaty agreed in 1389, Northumberland enjoyed a further period of eleven years of relative peace. There was some instability with the deposal of Richard II and replacement by Henry IV in 1399, because the Percy family, including Hotspur, played a significant role in the raising to power of the new king. In Scotland there were also disagreements between the nobility which culminated in George Dunbar, Earl of March, deserting to the English side. This gave Henry the excuse to renew the war in 1400, but it was not until two years later that the war was effectively renewed. A raid into Berwickshire by March brought retaliation when Sir Patrick Hepburn of Hailes, Sir John Haliburton and Robert de Lawedre, led a force of 400 Scots into Northumberland. This small raiding force was ambushed at Nisbet Muir by March and annihilated with Sir Patrick Hepburn being killed and other commanders captured.

The Scots retaliated once again with Archibald, 4th Earl of Douglas, organising a large force to mount a substantial raid into Northumberland. The raid was initially successful and got as far south as the Tyne without serious opposition but as it returned home via the Till Valley, laden with booty, they were caught and completely out-manoeuvred at Homildon Hill by an English force commanded by Sir Henry Percy; Hotspur had his revenge for Otterburn.

The Percys were by now the most powerful family in Northumberland and one of the most powerful in England. Just a year later, however, their relationship with the king they had helped place upon his throne had soured and Hotspur came out in rebellion against King Henry only to be killed at the Battle of Shrewsbury. His father, the earl, was caught up in a plot against the king two years afterwards and chose to flee the kingdom before returning after three years as a fugitive, only to be caught and slain in a skirmish at Bramham Moor in Yorkshire. Stripped of their possessions it was to be another eight years until the son of Hotspur had some of his family's lands restored. This was done as successive rulers of England discovered that loyalty to the Percy family ran deep in Northumberland, and their influence made it hard to govern effectively without them.

Despite the upheavals in the Percy family, these years were relatively peaceful for much of Northumberland, although there was still extensive skirmishing and small-time raiding on both sides of the border.

During the next few decades, however, there were events which shook and divided the nation. For the powerful Percy family, a bitter rivalry developed with the Neville family for the unofficial title of 'most powerful northern family'. The Nevilles were Yorkists, while the Percy family became closer to the Lancastrian royal court. In 1418, battle between the two factions erupted at the first Battle of St Albans resulting in a Yorkist victory and the death of the Earl of Northumberland. This battle heralded the beginning of the Wars of the Roses. This pattern continued over the next few decades. In 1461 the 3rd Earl of Northumberland was killed at the Battle of Towton and his son was captured. In the aftermath of Towton, Queen Margaret fled north into Northumberland where there were Lancastrian garrisons holding the castles of Alnwick, Bamburgh and Dunstanburgh. The queen quickly reached out to establish an alliance with Scotland in return for guaranteeing the return of Berwick to Scotland and the surrender of Carlisle. There was no chance of the surrender of Carlisle and after advancing from Northumberland to Durham with a small Lancastrian force support failed to materialise and Margaret failed to secure aid from France. Seeing weakness, the Yorkists moved against Northumberland and quickly secured the surrender of the garrisons at the three Lancastrian castles.

A year later there was a resurgence in the Lancastrian cause with the French King Louis XI providing Margaret with a small French army of between 2,000–6,000 men and a fleet to transport them. They landed at Bamburgh in October and quickly set about retaking the three castles which had been captured by the Yorkists. Margaret's fleet, however, was destroyed in a storm off Holy Island.

Edward IV reacted by advancing north with an army, but after falling ill he left it in the command of the Earl of Warwick and he set up his base at Warkworth. It seems that the native Lancastrian determination faltered at this point because Warwick was able to negotiate the surrender of Bamburgh and Dunstanburgh on Christmas Eve. Demonstrating a theme which was common in Northumberland during the Wars of the Roses, the commander of Dunstanburgh, Sir Ralph Percy (the 3rd Earl's younger brother) agreed to surrender the castle on the condition that he was allowed to remain in command of it and was also given command of Bamburgh.

The garrison at Alnwick remained loyal to the Lancastrian cause and refused to surrender, holding out until early the next year when a relief force from Scotland arrived. The Scots were too weak to take the battle to Warwick and it was agreed that the castle and town would be surrendered as long as the Lancastrian garrison could leave unmolested with their Scots allies. Warwick, misjudging the importance of Northumbrian influence and loyalty, appointed a Suffolk knight named Sir John Astley as commander overlooking the Northumbrian Sir Ralph Grey, whom he appointed deputy.

The situation did not last long. In March 1463 Sir Ralph Percy once again changed sides and allowed Scottish and French troops to enter both Bamburgh and Dunstanburgh castles. Just weeks later Sir Ralph Grey also turned, capturing Sir John Astley and handing over Alnwick to a Lancastrian commander. By June a Scottish force was besieging Norham Castle, and this brought the Earl of Warwick northwards once more. His larger force easily defeated the Scots and this caused Queen Margaret to admit defeat and return to France with her son. By December truces had been agreed, but the Duke of Somerset once again changed his allegiance back to the Lancastrian cause and made it to Bamburgh.

In 1646 Somerset went on the offensive and launched an attack on Yorkist strongholds in southern Northumberland, capturing the Tynedale castles of Bywell, Hexham, Langley, and Prudhoe. Somerset was now in a position to threaten Newcastle and cut off any future attempts to extend the truce with Scotland. At the same time as this was occurring, John Neville, Lord Montague, was riding northwards with a small body of men to negotiate just such an extension. He managed to avoid being ambushed near Newcastle and quickly rallied a force of several thousand to his banner and advanced through Northumberland. Near Wooler, his force met in battle with a Lancastrian force led by Somerset. The Battle of Hedgeley Moor ended in a decisive Yorkist victory, during which Sir Ralph Percy was killed.

Somerset knew the situation was dire but believed it could be retrieved if he moved into Tynedale and raise further men before engaging Montagu once more. By 15 May, Somerset had gathered approximately 5,000 men and was established in Tynedale near Hexham.

Lord Montagu was aware that his Lancastrian foe, the Duke of Somerset, had raised a small army in Tynedale and was based around Hexham. By mid-May 1664 Montagu had raised a smaller army of approximately 3,000 men at Newcastle and marched west to confront his foe. As he advanced into Tynedale, Montagu received reports of the enemy dispositions and information that Henry VI was in the town of Hexham. The Yorkists crossed the River Tyne on the night of 12–13 May, and by the morning of 14 May they were preparing for an attack on Hexham.

Somerset's forces were encamped at Linnel's Bridge over the fast-flowing Devil's Water, just to the south of Hexham, and the speedy Yorkist advance had taken them by surprise. Somerset quickly organised his forces and deployed in three detachments in a meadow bordering the burn. The Lancastrians had the burn at their backs and their left flank was protected by a small wood. Somerset commanded the middle detachment, Lord Roos the right flank, and Sir Ralph Grey the left.

Montagu also arrayed his force in three detachments. He commanded the middle, Lord Willoughby the right and Lord Greystoke the left. The Yorkists occupied higher ground and the Lancastrians had no sooner deployed then Montagu ordered the charge. Once again, Lord Roos failed the test of battle and his detachment broke and fled into Hexham. This allowed Montagu to outflank the Yorkists and a short but bloody battle developed. Morale collapsed and the Lancastrians were pushed backwards into the Devil's Water, with many drowning or being crushed to death as they tried to climb the steep banks. The majority made for Dipton Wood and were subsequently captured. Somerset attempted to fight his way out, but after being unhorsed and wounded he took shelter in a cottage, where he was discovered and captured. Henry VI had been in Hexham and was able to flee.

The Yorkists then advanced into Hexham and on the evening following the battle, Montagu ordered the execution of thirty of the leading Lancastrian prisoners. These included Somerset and Lord Roos. Days later a survivor of the battle, Sir William Tailboys, was captured hiding in a coal mine near Newcastle with £2,000 from Henry VI's war chest. He was also executed, and Montagu used the money to pay his army. This defeat effectively ended the Lancastrian cause for the next few years.

The Lancastrian castles in Tynedale were quickly retaken and Montagu set about attacking Alnwick, Bamburgh and Dunstaburgh using siege guns. Alnwick and Dunstanburgh surrendered on 23 and 24 July 1464 but Bamburgh, under the command of Sir Ralph Grey (who must have survived Hexham), resisted and had to be stormed. Grey was captured and, as he was accounted a traitor, taken to Doncaster for trial and subsequent execution.

Alnwick Castle

Alnwick Castle, known as 'The Windsor of the North', is one of the most majestic castles in Britain. It stands at the northern end of the town (which itself features many medieval remains) on top of a steep bank of the River Aln. Alnwick was handed over to a Gilbert de Tesson after the

Alnwick Castle with the Percy Lion in foreground (© Michael Conrad/Adobe Stock)

Approach to Alnwick Castle (Courtesy of Jody Walker)

Norman conquest. It was rumoured that Gilbert had been King William's standard bearer at the Battle of Hastings, but regardless of the veracity of this, Gilbert held Alnwick until 1096 when he supported Earl Robert de Mowbray's rebellion and was sequestrated.

The next holder was Ivo de Vescy, 1st Baron of Alnwick, and he constructed the first motte and bailey castle on the site above the river. His only child, a daughter named Beatrix, married a Eustace fitz John. At the time, England was in the grip of the civil war known as the Anarchy, with the country torn between support for Stephen of Blois and the Empress Matilda. Eustace threw his support behind the latter and, foreseeing the forthcoming strife, immediately set about fortifying his home by surrounding the wooden motte and bailey with a stone curtain wall, followed by a keep consisting of several stone towers.

David I of Scotland supported Matilda (largely to cause trouble in the neighbouring realm, but also with the hope and ambition of re-establishing his claims to part, or all, of Northumberland and possibly Cumberland) and Eustace marched alongside him to fight Stephen's forces, only to be defeated at the Battle of the Standard in 1138. Eustace may not have been successful in battle, but he was obviously more successful in matters of diplomacy as he was soon able to make his peace with Stephen.

Eustace's son, William, inherited Alnwick from his father, but chose to use his mother's name and became William de Vescy. His son, named after his grandfather, succeeded in 1184 and was one of the barons who was appointed to enforce the observance of Magna Carta in 1215. Eustace joined the rebel nobles against King John and paid homage to the king of Scotland; a year later his castle was burned in retribution, although the damage was superficial.

Misfortune befell the de Vescys two generations

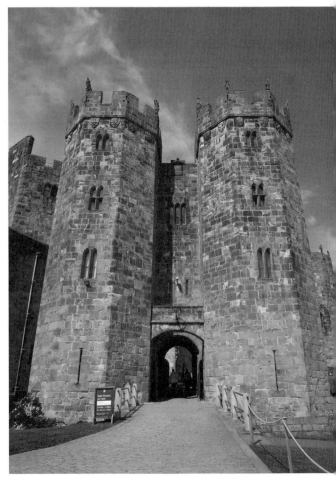

Alnwick Castle Gatehouse (Courtesy of Jody Walker)

later in 1265 when John de Vescy rebelled against King Henry III and had his castle at Alnwick forfeited for a number of years. Although back at Alnwick, the de Vescy star was waning, with John succeeded by his younger brother William in 1288. William died in 1297 and left behind only an illegitimate son named William de Vescy of Kildare. Because the illegitimate could not claim the property of Alnwick Castle or the title of Baron of Alnwick, the castle was granted to Anthony Bek, the Prince Bishop of Durham and a favourite of King Edward I.

Alnwick Castle (Courtesy of Jody Walker)

Alnwick was such a strong redoubt that it was largely left untouched by the early Anglo-Scottish wars although the countryside around was ravaged on numerous occasions. Bek was a notorious soldier-priest but seems to have been more than willing to get rid of his Alnwick property (perhaps because he was also the owner of Norham Castle), and in 1309 he sold it to Lord Henry Percy beginning an association with the Percys which goes on to this day.

Henry's descendants had originated in a village in Normandy called Percee (meaning forest glade); a William de Percy had been a part of William I's entourage and had been rewarded with lands in southern and central England. Henry had spent most of his time in Yorkshire but had seen extensive service on the Borders in the wars against Sir William Wallace, being rewarded with large estates in Scotland. Henry rebuilt the castle keeping to much of the original plan, but adding a great many new buildings such as a great hall.

His son, also named Henry, succeeded in 1315 (the year of Bannockburn) and immediately ordered the construction of the two octagonal towers which flank the gatehouse. The second Lord Henry, for all the improvements he had made at Alnwick, preferred the greater comfort of Warkworth Castle and spent much of this time there while Alnwick was largely the province of the March Warden.

A fighting family, the Percy lords saw a great deal of action on the border and even in France, but Henry, 4th Lord Percy, oversaw a decline in the family fortunes after he and his son, another Henry (nicknamed Hotspur), rebelled firstly against King Richard II, and then against King Henry IV. After Hotspur was slain in battle against the king in 1403, his father went on the run before returning to fight – only to be killed in 1409.

At this point, Alnwick passed into the hands of John of Lancaster and he held it for five years until Henry V decided it was too difficult to govern Northumberland effectively without the presence of the Percy family, so great was their influence. As a result, he awarded Alnwick to Hotspur's son, naming him Henry, 2nd Earl of Northumberland. Henry had a number of burdens placed upon him, foremost among them was his position as General Warden of the Marches. This position resulted in him being a prime target for both the Scots and the more troublesome elements among his own Northumbrians. Alnwick Castle once again proved to be too strong to be assailed, but the town did not escape so lightly, being burned twice in 1424 and 1428. As a result of this the crown granted a licence to encircle the town with a protective wall in 1434. The wall, featuring four gates, was eventually completed. One of the gates and its guard tower, Bondgate and Hotspur Tower, still survive, while another, Pottergate, was rebuilt in the eighteenth century. The remaining two gates, Bailiffgate and Clayport, have, unfortunately, disappeared with the passage of time.

The next earl was killed fighting for the Lancastrians in the Wars of the Roses and the castle was taken over by Lord Montagu. The castle changed hands on no less than four occasions during the Wars of the Roses, but by the end was still a Yorkist stronghold in the hands of Lord Montagu. King Edward IV, however, also found it difficult to govern Northumberland without the Percy influence and, also concerned with the growing power of Montagu and his brother, the Earl of Warwick, sacked Montagu and restored Alnwick and the earldom to yet another Henry Percy, 4th Earl of Northumberland, in 1469. This earl remained in his seat for twenty years, but was slain by a mob as he tried to enforce an unpopular royal tax in Yorkshire.

Alnwick Castle (© g8ste/Adobe Stock)

Directions

Alnwick Castle, Alnwick, Northumberland, NE66 1NG

Tel: 01665 511 100

www.alnwickcastle.com

Car – Alnwick Castle is less than a mile off the A1 and is well signposted. The main castle car park is just off Denwick Lane (B1340); the postcode for the car park is NE66 1YU (parking charge is £3 per vehicle for the day and open from 10 am during the season).

Train – the East Coast mainline from London to Edinburgh stops at Alnmouth station, which is four miles from Alnwick. A taxi or bus (X18) can be taken from Alnmouth station (a journey of approximately 10 minutes).

Bus – there are bus stops and a bus station in the centre of Alnwick, with buses connecting Alnwick to the surrounding towns as well as the city of Newcastle (the X15 and X18 buses both run from Haymarket bus station). It is approximately a 5-minute walk to the castle from the bus station.

Norham Castle

The massive and much fought over castle at Norham was founded in 1121 by Ranulph Flambard, Prince Bishop of Durham. At the time Norham was not actually a part of Northumberland, it was a part of Norhamshire and Islandshire, belonging to the Prince Bishops of Durham.

Norham has a surprising number of romantic associations for a castle with such a bloody and dramatic history. Not only does the castle feature extensively in Sir Walter Scott's epic poem *Marmeon*, it is also the subject of an 1845 oil painting, *Norham Castle, Sunrise*, by William Turner which is currently in the collection of the Tate (Turner also painted and drew Norham on several other occasions).

The castle, as could be expected of one belonging to the Prince Bishops of Durham, was not only an essential part of border defence protecting a vital crossing point of the River Tweed on the very border between England and Scotland, but was also the administrative centre for the territory of Norhamshire and Islandshire. As such, Norham was palatial and was suitable for accommodating royalty and playing a role in high diplomacy between the two countries. Given its position and importance, it comes as no surprise that Norham saw its share of bloodshed and strife. The castle itself was besieged on at least nine occasions (being successfully captured four times) before being largely destroyed in 1513, shortly before the Battle of Flodden. The remains are now a curious mix of the layout of the original medieval fortifications and the rebuild after 1513, which turned Norham into an early example of a Tudor border-fortress for gunpowder artillery.

Norham first saw action when it was besieged on two occasions in the twelfth century as successive Scottish kings attempted to press their claim on Northumberland and Cumberland. After this there was a short period of peace which was still overshadowed by distrust. In 1153 King Henry II ordered the then Prince Bishop, Hugh de Puiset, to rebuild the castle. Hugh was an enthusiastic builder who went about his schemes on a grand scale. His work at Norham, between 1157–70, included the building of the Great Tower, the inner-ward gatehouse and the west gate. Hugh was also responsible for the building of the chancel at St Cuthbert's

Church in Norham. This remains an outstanding and fascinating example of Romanesque church architecture in Northumberland.

The castle was further enhanced by substantial spending by King John between 1208–12. This improved the outer ward and constructed the sheep gate as well as other unspecified elements of the castle. This was perhaps just as well, as the Scottish King Alexander II laid siege to Norham in 1215 but was unsuccessful. The subsequent peace between the two nations was signed at Norham four years later.

Peace then came once again to Norham, but the castle was maintained and this peace was overshadowed in 1291 after the deaths of the Scottish King Alexander III and his young daughter and heir. Norham was once again thrust into the limelight when, in May 1291, it hosted King Edward I and his entourage as he arbitrated between the claimants to the Scottish crown. The occasion was an extremely lavish affair with Bishop Anthony Bek ensuring that all were awed by the power of the English king. To house the king, an impressive hall house was built in the inner ward. The arbitration, which continued into the next year, must have required the

Norham Castle (Martin Norman / CC BY 2.0 https://commons.wikimedia.org/wiki/File:Norham_Castle.jpg)

construction of a great deal of temporary accommodation as Edward was attended upon by sixty-seven northern magnates and their entourages. Such was the scale of the meetings that in 1292 the royal household at Norham required the use of 269 horses.

Norham was so strong that Robert the Bruce ignored it during his invasions of 1311 and 1312. In 1318 (four years after the Scots victory at Bannockburn) he laid siege to the castle for a year, but succeeded in capturing only the outer ward – and this was retaken after a few days. The castle's constable during this time, Sir Thomas Grey of Heton, earned the respect, grudging though it might have been, of King Robert for his success in denying the Scots. It was unsuccessfully besieged again in 1319 (a siege which lasted for seven months) and yet again in 1322. In 1327 the Scots were successful in taking the castle, but the Treaty of Northampton returned the castle the next year.

After this, Northumberland slowly recovered, but Norham was extensively repaired and remodelled with the Great Tower being reconstructed to resemble a substantial fortified tower house. The castle was substantially remodelled throughout the fifteenth century, although the castle played only a minor role in the Wars of the Roses. Under the reign of King Edward IV the castle housed gunpowder bombards and cannon, and Bishop Fox renewed the moat in 1494. In 1497 the castle was once again besieged by the Scots and the bombardment caused substantial damage requiring extensive repairs. The last of these, the completion of the two-storey west gate, was completed in 1512.

Just a year later the castle was taken once more, and a massive amount of damage done by artillery with the Great Tower being partly brought down. The Scots victory did not last long as they were defeated just weeks later at Flodden. Once again, urgent repairs were undertaken at Norham. This rebuilding, which included the construction of Clapham's Tower, changed the castle into a platform for the new gunpowder technology, and by 1523 there was a garrison of twenty gunners (including experts from Portsmouth), seventy archers and a hundred horsemen, but there were also indications of a lack of care of some of the buildings in the fort. Strengthening continued over the next thirty-six years, but when Bishop Tunstall refused to take the Oath of Supremacy in 1559, Queen Elizabeth I took possession of Norhamshire, including Norham Castle.

The ancient castle continued to be used by the wardens of the East March, but by 1569 it was being condemned as being unfit for the habitation of the garrison, and by 1594 it was in such a ruinous state that there were only two habitable rooms in the entire complex. Two years later the parsimonious queen took the decision to spend no more on Norham.

Following the union of the crowns in 1603 Norham lost any purpose and the ruins passed through many hands until they were placed under the guardianship of the state in 1923. Since 1984 the castle has been in the care of English Heritage.

Any visit to Norham Castle should always be complemented by a visit to St Cuthbert's Church in Norham village. The Norman church is interesting both architecturally and historically and was where King Edward I received homage from the competitors for the Scottish crown. The church was also fortified by Robert the Bruce and used as a stronghold from which to lay siege to the castle. The large churchyard is also worth a look. It reputedly contains the body of St Ceolwulf (former King of Northumbria) and also contains the grave of Corporal Daniel Logan Laidlaw, VC, the famed Piper of Loos from the First World War.

Directions
Car – 6 miles south-west of Berwick-upon-Tweed, on minor road (signposted) off B6470 (Sat Nav: TD15 2JY).
Bus – Perryman's service 67 runs regularly from Berwick Station (20 mins).
Train – Nearest station is Berwick-upon-Tweed.

Prices
Free admission.

Facilities
Car park and small shop on site. Note that some of the ground is uneven and prone to becoming muddy, not suitable for wheelchairs.

Opening Times
April – September: 10 am – 5 pm

Warkworth Castle

The pretty coastal village of Warkworth at the mouth of the beautiful River Coquet has been used as a defensive site since the Stone Age but found fame during the medieval period. The Coquet bends sharply at Warkworth and this bend meant that the site was easily defensible. It was probably the Votadini tribe who first fortified the site before the coming of the Romans, and this was later replaced by an Anglo-Saxon stronghold. In the early eighth century, King Ceolwulf of Northumbria founded a church at Warkworth and gifted the stronghold to the monks of Lindisfarne when he abdicated to take up the monastic life. This charitable gift did not last long as King Osbert revoked the monks' grant, but was killed in 855 and twenty years later the settlement and fort was sacked by Viking raiders.

At some point in the eleventh century, one of the early earls of Northumberland built a motte and bailey castle at the site. The result of this was a further boon for the church when Earl Robert de Mowbray presented the tithes from the village to the monks at Tynemouth Priory (which he had recently founded).

After the Battle of the Standard in 1138, King Stephen granted the earldom of Northumberland to Prince Henry, the son of the defeated king of Scots. The prince oversaw a period of over a decade of prosperous and peaceful growth in Northumberland and he made several improvements at Warkworth, including the construction of a stone curtain wall and improvement to the bailey. After Henry died in 1152 his son, William, took over, but it was only six years before King Henry II decreed that Northumberland would henceforth become, once more, an English-run possession and granted the earldom to Roger fitz Richard. Unsurprisingly this angered Prince William and in 1162 he made his first attempt to recover Northumberland; eleven years later he succeeded in taking back Warkworth Castle but was defeated and taken prisoner at Alnwick just a year later.

After the death of Roger fitz Richard the earldom came to Robert fitz Roger. In 1199 he relocated to Warkworth from the south of England where he became very invested in Northumberland affairs. Just four years after he moved to Warkworth he was made sheriff of Northumberland and King John granted him lands at Rothbury and Corbridge. With his new-found

Warkworth Castle from the Air (© Craig/Adobe Stock)

wealth and influence, Robert improved the castle at Warkworth. The curtain wall was massively improved and the Carrickfergus Tower was constructed along with the gatehouse. The hall-house, where Robert lived, was substantially improved and a chapel was also built in the grounds. Robert also made more general improvements by deepening the moat around the castle.

Robert's descendants took the surname Clavering, and continued to improve the castle throughout the thirteenth century with the chronicler Matthew Paris describing Warkworth as being a 'noble castle' by the middle of the century, and the castle was graced by a royal visit when King Edward I spent one night here in 1292.

By this time, however, the Claverings were experiencing some financial problems and these were worsened by the outbreak of the Anglo-Scottish wars in 1296. The wars meant that the castle had to be occupied by more troops. Such were the financial problems of the Claverings that in

Panoramic view of Warkworth from the River Coquet (© thecoach1/Adobe Stock)

1311 the king agreed to take partial responsibility for Warkworth, taking it, and other Northumbrian properties, off their hands in exchange for lands in southern England. Some of these soldiers were provided by the king, and by 1319 the castle was occupied by a garrison of twenty-four soldiers (half of them being provided by the royal purse). These measures were shown to be necessary as Warkworth was twice besieged by the Scots in 1327.

By 1332 the crown was completely in control of Warkworth after the last of the Clavering family died. However, it was evident that it was difficult for a far-distant crown to exert sufficient control over the northern castle and in the same year King Edward III granted Warkworth to the lord of Alnwick, Henry de Percy II. Warkworth remained the principal family seat of the Percys until 1576.

The Percy family divided their time between their castle at Alnwick and the newly acquired Warkworth Castle and spent considerable time on improving both the living standards and the fortifications. These improvements included the building of the Grey Mare's Tail Tower. In the fourteenth century, the 1st Earl of Northumberland, Henry de Percy IV, paid for the construction of the magnificent and imposing keep. The 1st earl, however, was overly ambitious and, after helping to overthrow King Richard II, he rebelled against King Henry IV in 1403. His famous son and heir, known widely as Henry Hotspur, was killed in battle at Shrewsbury and the royal army besieged Warkworth, battering the old castle with cannon fire until the defenders were forced to surrender. The earl himself was killed in battle five years after his son, and the family estates were forfeited to the crown.

Henry IV appointed his son, John, Duke of Bedford, as his commander in the north, and he spent considerable time at Warkworth, but it became increasingly clear that the people of Northumberland were used to the power of the Percy family and Henry V gave the family its lands back. The 2nd Earl was none other than the son of Hotspur, another Henry Percy. Clearly a pious man with an awareness of his family's past, he was responsible for the planning of the building of the collegiate church in the outer bailey of Warkworth (likely he was going to use the church as a family mausoleum), but despite the warnings of his family history, this was never finished because he was killed fighting for the Lancastrians during the Wars of the Roses. The 3rd Earl was also killed in battle, at the Battle of Towton and the Yorkists captured Warkworth.

Once more the Percy's were disinherited, with Warkworth and the earldom passing to John Neville. It was during this phase that construction began on the Montague Tower at the south east of the castle, but once again the crown, this time in the person of King Edward IV, found it difficult to maintain sufficient control over Northumberland without the Percy family. John Neville agreed to change his title to Marquess Montague when the king made a fourth Percy Earl of Northumberland in 1471. Despite the claims that the people of Northumberland were fiercely loyal to the Percys, it would seem some of his more southerly tenants were not so loyal and he was murdered when he tried to enforce an unpopular tax.

Despite the unfortunate end of his father, the 5th earl, who was known as 'the Magnificent', preferred to live on his estates in Yorkshire. Despite this, he oversaw added significantly to the castle by overseeing the building of the Lion Tower and made living improvements to the hall house and keep. His descendants, however, exercised greater interest in the old castle, making lengthy visits to the site. Indeed, the 6th earl, another Henry, made substantial repairs to the curtain wall, the gatehouse and the Montague Tower. Family disputes, however, led to Warkworth Castle being left to the crown when the 6th Earl died in 1537 and, although the castle was kept in a state of adequate repair, it had lost much of its importance and lustre.

For twenty years the castle was the residence of the border wardens, but even when possession was returned to the Percy family in 1557, not one of the 7th, 8th or 9th Earls of Northumberland were to live there. The 7th Earl was beheaded after he rebelled during the Rising of the North in 1569 and his descendants spent many of their years in captivity, and even when freed, were forbidden to live on their northern estates.

In 1604 the castle was leased to Sir Ralph Grey, though it is hard to see why as he showed very little interest in the castle and it fell into ruin, with a survey four years later describing all of the buildings except the keep as being ruinous. At this time the magnificent site was being used as an open cattle pen, and ten years later the keep was used as a grain store. During the Civil War in the 1640s the castle was occupied on two occasions, once by the Scots and once by Cromwell's parliamentary army.

Ironically, the end of the castle came at the hands of a Percy. In 1672, the widow of the 11th Earl allowed the estate auditor to use the remains as a quarry for the manor house which he was building for himself at Chirton, near North Shields. His use of the stone from the site left it as a ruin, picturesque but uninhabitable. It was not until the 4th Duke, Admiral Algernon Percy (1792–1865), that the site was made habitable again. The admiral oversaw repairs to the keep and made the top floor habitable. The 8th Duke, Alan Percy (1880–1930), placed the castle and its environs under the control of the Ministry of Works eight years before his death. It was subsequently taken over by English Heritage.

A visit to Warkworth should not only include the castle, for there is much more of interest in the village. The village church is probably the finest example of a Norman church in Northumberland and contains much of great interest, while a short walk down the road to the east of the church brings the visitor to one of the few remaining English examples of a fortified bridge (c. fourteenth century).

A walk downstream from the castle is also well worthwhile. The views of the castle and the beautiful River Coquet are marvellous and as you walk the half mile past the old deer park, you come to the site across from the hidden and little-known Warkworth Hermitage. Between April and September it is possible to take a boat across to the hermitage and it is certainly well worth the trip. Once you have got out of the boat, a short flight of rough-hewn stone steps take one up to chambers which have been cut into the rock. These include both a chapel and sacristy, and the whole structure is a moving testimony to the piety of the fourteenth century.

Warkworth Castle Keep (Draco2008 CC BY 2.0 https://commons.wikimedia.org/w/index.php?curid=12612749)

Clearly the majority of the hermits who lived here throughout the period had the support of the Percys, and by the 1530s the resident hermit, George Lancastre, was receiving a salary of £13 6s 8d (almost £8,000 today) and was also the 6th earl's agent on the Warkworth estate.

Directions
Car – 7½ miles south of Alnwick on the A1068. There is parking available at the castle (£3.10 refundable upon admission to the castle), and additional paid parking in the village. (Sat-Nav: NE65 0UJ)

Public Transport (Bus) – Arriva service X18 runs hourly from Newcastle via Morpeth, Alnmouth Station and Warkworth to Berwick.

Train – Regular services run on the East Coast Main Line from stations including Newcastle Central and Edinburgh.

Prices
Adult: £6.80 (Hermitage: £4.50)
Child (5–17): £4.10 (Hermitage: £3.00)
Concession: £6.10 (Hermitage: £4.10)
Family (two adults and up to three children): £17.70 (Hermitage: £13.00)

Facilities

The on-site shop sells a range of English Heritage products and souvenirs along with ice-cream, tea, coffee, and hot chocolate. While there are no tables, visitors are welcome to picnic on grassed areas. Dogs are permitted (on a lead) and there are toilets on site. The nearby village of Warwkorth features a number of hotels, public houses and cafes which offer a wide variety of food and refreshments.

Opening Times

See English Heritage website: https://www.english-heritage.org.uk/visit/places/warkworth-castle-and-hermitage/prices-and-opening-times/

Brinkburn Abbey

Many Northumbrian nobles of the twelfth century were anxious for their souls and one way they saw of gaining their rightful place in heaven was by instituting and funding religious houses on parcels of land which they owned. At some point between 1130 and 1135, in the reign of Henry I, the Baron of Mitford, Sir William Bertram I (d.1152), agreed to found a priory for Augustinian canons. Sir William had married into the influential de Balliol family and was obviously keen to follow the example of other important nobles.

He chose a very beautiful and secluded location for the site, which lay in deep woodland in the bend of the River Coquet. Local superstition alluded to a fairy graveyard at the site. Although concealed, the site was vulnerable to attack and had little or no adequate defensive fortifications. The founding brothers came from the monastery of St Mary de Insula, at Pentney Priory in Norfolk, and they were led by the first prior, Ralph. The church and manor house still survive, but excavations have shown that the charter house and the cellar of the manor house were extremely robust structures which may have been used as refuges for the brothers in the event of danger.

The existing church structure is largely from the end of the twelfth century, and experts believe the construction process took over thirty years. It would seem that the original church was dedicated to St Peter, but by the

Brinkburn Priory (R) and Manor House (L) (JohnArmagh / CC-BY-SA-4.0)

reign of Henry II (beginning in December 1154) it had been rededicated to St Peter and St Paul. Any newly founded religious house needed land so that it could raise funds to support itself, and Brinkburn Priory was no exception. In the original grants of land was a broad swathe of land north of the Coquet. This land grant extended from the Black Burn in the west to Weldon in the east.

When Sir William died he was succeeded by his son Roger, and this son made a further endowment when he gifted the church at Felton to the priory, and the lands of the priory developed into a scattered domain, but unfortunately for the brothers, Brinkburn Priory was never wealthy. Charters of confirmation were granted to the priory in 1200, by King John, and by Henry III in 1252. For these charters the prior had to agree to pay the crown the sum of 10 marks, but such was the claimed 'penury' of the priory, that the sum went unpaid for many years. In 1292, before the Scottish wars, the priory had been valued at £31 (almost £26,000 today), but in common with the rest of Northumberland, this value was to be badly affected by the wars.

Due to innumerable Scottish invasions during the period of the Scottish wars, and particularly after the Scottish victory at Bannockburn, the priory was repeatedly the target for raiders. By 1322 the house was in such a state that the prior and canons wrote to King Edward II to petition him to relieve the losses they had suffered at the hands of the Scots (and, probably, of English marauders). By this time the repeated raids and the danger of the siting of Brinkburn meant that the numbers of canons had declined markedly to just twelve. There is no record of the king providing such relief but his successor, King Edward III, reacted by providing aid on two occasions, in 1333 and 1334, but this does not seem to have helped to relieve the penury of the priory because the prior wrote to the bishop in 1391 complaining of the poverty of the house.

Brinkburn's monetary situation does not seem to have improved; records of 1419 mention the priory as having been robbed of its books, charters, chalices, ornaments, vestments and other valuable goods. The bishop responded to this sacrilege by demanding the return of the items within twenty days, but as they were never returned, it seems that no one listened to him.

The misfortunes of Brinkburn were not over as the priory also became a target for Scottish border reivers. On one occasion it was said that the raiders could not locate the priory and, thinking they had been spared, the canons began ringing the church bells in celebration of their deliverance. Unfortunately, the reivers were still in the area and simply followed the sound of the bells to the church, which was, again, ransacked. Tales of missing treasure abound at the site and in 1834 a party of workmen discovered a large hoard of gold coins dating back to the reigns of Edward II (1308–27) and Richard II (1377–99). There are also tales of a hidden hoard concealed by the canons in the waters of the River Coquet beside the priory.

By 1535 the priory was valued at £69 (over £58,000), but when the priory was dissolved the next year (all minor houses assessed at less than £200 suffered this fate) the official valuation was given at £95 (almost £77,000). Brinkburn was left neglected and began to fall into ruin,

Stained Glass Window at Brinkburn Priory (© philipbird123/Adobe Stock)

although some attempt was made at restoration in the 1830s. In the nineteenth century the owner, Major Cadogan Hodgson, funded a very sympathetic restoration (famed local architect John Dobson had undertaken some of the earlier work).

During the early restoration work on 25 July 1834 some workmen were removing the remains of a burnt-out wooden building when one of them discovered a 3 inch x 6 inch brass vessel which contained hundreds of coins, including gold nobles from the reign of Edward III and Richard II. It is probable that the coins were hidden at some point between 1380 and 1390. Interestingly, a similar find of coins had taken place at nearby Fenwick Tower in June 1775.

Today, Brinkburn is a remarkably peaceful and tranquil place which is owned and maintained by English Heritage. The church is one of the best examples of early Gothic architecture in the north of England.

Directions

Car – 4½ miles south-east of the beautiful village of Rothbury, the turn-off for Brinkburn is clearly signposted on the B6344 (Sat-Nav: NE65 8AR). There is a free car park on site.

Bus – Arriva service X14 runs regularly from Newcastle to Thropton via Morpeth and Rothbury. Nearest stop is Brinkburn New Houses which necessitates a walk of approximately 1½ miles along the roadside.

Prices
Adult: £4.90
Child (5–17): £2.90
Concession: £4.40
Family (two adults and up to three children): £12.70

Facilities
The on-site shop sells a range of English Heritage products and souvenirs along with ice-cream, tea, coffee, and hot chocolate. There are a number of picnic benches on the grassy areas of the grounds and visitors are welcome to bring a picnic while the spacious grounds are welcoming to children and families. Dogs are permitted (on a lead) and there are toilets on site.

Opening Times
30 March – 30 September
Monday – Tuesday: closed
Wednesday – Sunday: 10 am – 6 pm

1 October – 28 October
Monday–Friday: closed
Saturday–Sunday: 10 am – 4 pm

29 October – 4 November
Monday–Sunday: 10 am – 4 pm

Battle of Otterburn, 1388

As a result of the almost constant fighting between England and Scotland, a fierce and bitter rivalry had developed between the Percy and the Douglas families. In the summer of 1388 James, 2nd Earl of Douglas, led a substantial raid on Northumberland and Cumberland. Douglas probably suspected that Henry Percy, 1st Earl of Northumberland and newly appointed Warden of the East March, would not be able to stop his force as he was in dispute with other powerful English nobles, and Northumberland was already considerably weakened by previous raids. While the main force headed

Battle of Otterburn by G. Kollidas (© Georgios Kollidas/Adobe Stock)

for Carlisle, Douglas ravaged the countryside in Northumberland, around Newcastle and into Durham before retreating northwards. The Scots did not attempt to take Newcastle, whose defence was led by Percy's son, Sir Henry 'Hotspur' Percy, as they realised its defences were too strong, but during either a skirmish or a single combat, Douglas had unhorsed Hotspur and captured his pennon. To add insult to injury Douglas promised to return to Scotland with the pennon and fly it from Dalkeith Castle.

The Scots retreated northwards along the line of the modern A696 and on the evening of 19 August made camp approximately a mile west of the village of Otterburn. Douglas probably suspected that Hotspur would attempt a pursuit and apparently ordered a watch be kept and the construction of rudimentary defensive positions. Douglas knew his man. Hotspur left Newcastle with a force estimated at 8,000, including men-at-arms, archers and others. Many of his force were mounted and Hotspur made an impressive 30-mile forced march north. Unfortunately, scouts told Hotspur that the Scottish force numbered only 3,000, when in fact it was approximately double this figure and Hotspur determined to act immediately, making a moonlit assault without waiting for further reinforcement.

However, Hotspur had taken the Scots by surprise. They had settled down for the night and did not expect an attack at so late an hour, but Hotspur, instead of rushing the Scots, decided to deploy his men in formation and make a plan of attack and this allowed many of the Scots, though by no means all, to draw up in defensive formations to the east of their camp.

Hotspur dispatched a strong force to flank the Scots. Under the command of either Thomas Umfraville or Sir Matthew Redman (accounts differ), the force took a wide detour to the north through heavily wooded ground and were substantially delayed. The main English force, led by Hotspur, made a direct assault on the Scots lines but Douglas, who had previously scouted the ground, led a flanking attack which fell on the northern flank of Hotspur's force. At approximately this time the English flanking attack reached the Scots camp but found it largely deserted and its commander ordered his men back to their original positions. Remarkably, he failed to hear the clash of battle taking place just a few hundred metres to the east.

Douglas's flank attack succeeded in turning the English line even though Douglas himself was killed; in the fierce fighting the English found themselves at a disadvantage, tired after their march and unable to utilise their longbowmen effectively in the darkness. Hotspur and his brother, Ralph, were captured along with a significant number of other English knights. The English retreated in good order and managed to beat off an attempted Scottish attack capturing several hundred men but, despite the loss of Douglas, it remained a Scottish victory.

Highly Inaccurate Account of the Battle of Otterburn (Public Domain)

Directions

Car – the supposed site of the Battle of Otterburn is clearly signposted off the main A696 road and there is limited car parking at the site, which is marked by an information board.

Battle of Homildon Hill, 1402

After the Battle of Otterburn the ill-feeling between England and Scotland continued to simmer with frequent raids and skirmishes. The Scots were ever-quick to take advantage of instability in England which drew the attention of the London government away from the northern border. In 1402 Henry IV was the newly crowned king of England and the nobility was still divided; the Scottish King Robert III viewed him with disdain as a usurper and continued to refer to him officially as the Duke of Lancaster. In the spring, a Welsh revolt led by Owain Glyndŵr had broken out and Henry became distracted by this crisis.

Determined to take advantage, Sir Archibald, 4th Earl of Douglas, led a strong force of 10,000 Scots across the border, once again looting and pillaging as far as Newcastle. Loaded down with booty, the Scots slowly withdrew to the north after what they no doubt viewed as a successful raid. However, there was discord in Scotland as well and the rallying English forces under the command of the Earl of Northumberland (who was also Lord Marshal) and his son, Henry 'Hotspur' Percy, were offered aid and advice by the Scotsman, George Dunbar, Earl of March.

Dunbar advised that the Scots were retreating along the road from Wooler to the border at Coldstream. He also advised the earl and his son to lie in wait for his countrymen at a site to the north of Wooler. The English force, which was probably around equal in number to the Scots, was at Bamburgh and the Percys made a forced march to cut the Scots off. The Scots initially camped on Milfield Plain, but an English attempt to attack was spotted and the Scots took up a strong position on Homildon Hill.

Hotspur, no doubt chafing from his defeat at Otterburn, was still possessed of his impetuosity and urged an attack uphill but, luckily for him, the Earl of March took a cooler view and persuaded the Percys to instead utilise their longbowmen. The Percys promptly dispatched their archers to Harehope Hill where they could shoot onto the Scots, but could not be charged due to the deep ravine between the two hills. The Scottish massed ranks of pike and spearmen (in the formation known as a schiltron) were hugely vulnerable to the storm of arrows; Douglas seems to have been paralysed and unsure as to what action to take and casualties mounted rapidly. The Scots then attempted to use their own bowmen to attack the longbowmen, but found they were out of range and the Scots archers subsequently fled the field.

At this point Douglas attempted to lead a detachment to attack the longbowmen on Harehope Hill, but was frustrated by the terrain and suffered critical losses as the longbowmen continued to pour fire into the Scots ranks.

Two knights, one being Sir John Swinton of that Ilk, decided to lead a charge against the main English body, with Sir John apparently stating that it was better to die in melee than be shot down like a deer. However, the charge failed and most were killed by the arrows of the longbowmen. Witnessing this failure, the remaining Scots routed with many subsequently drowning as they tried to cross the River Tweed. The Scots suffered heavy casualties while English losses were said to be very low. Many of the surviving Scots nobles were taken prisoner including Douglas, his brother George, 1st Earl of Angus, and Thomas Dunbar, 5th Earl of Moray.

For Hotspur it must have been a sweet revenge for the defeat at Otterburn, but it was to be soured by the ingratitude of King Henry. The Percys had been kept short of money by the king and hoped that the substantial ransoms would pay both themselves and their army, but Henry ordered the prisoners to be turned over to his custody. Furious at this perceived affront, Hotspur refused and instead released them after abstracting a promise that they would aid him in his future efforts against King Henry. Hotspur was true to his word and rebelled the next year, leading a large force to confront the king on the Welsh border; he was killed at the Battle of Shrewsbury on 21 July 1403.

Facilities

Homildon Hill (now called Humbleton Hill) is largely farmland and the site of the battle, which is within the boundaries of Northumberland National Park, is largely anonymous. A boulder known as the Bendor Stone was long thought to commemorate the site of the battle, but is in fact the remains of a Bronze Age standing stone. Humbleton itself lies just to the west off the A697 between Wooler and Akeld.

Morpeth Castle

Owned and managed by the Landmark Trust, a stay at Morpeth Castle allows the visitor to immerse themselves in the history of this fabulous county. Morpeth Castle was built in the twelfth century to replace an earlier castle which had been destroyed following the de Merlay family's decision to support a rebellion against King John. The motte of an earlier castle can be clearly seen to the south of the present castle.

In 1271 Morpeth passed from the hands of the de Merlays into those of the Greystokes. This family already had widespread interests in Cumbria and Northumberland and used the castle primarily to oversee their local properties, installing a constable and steward in the castle along with a small garrison.

The present accommodation is actually the gatehouse of this castle and it is likely that either the constable or steward resided on the upper floor of the very imposing gatehouse. This gatehouse replaced an earlier one and was constructed on the orders of Lord William Greystoke, the Good Baron, between 1342 and 1359. From the construction of the ground floor of the gatehouse it would appear that this area was used as some sort of courtroom, perhaps for the baron's court locally.

Morpeth Castle Gatehouse (Tzdelski13 / CC BY-SA 4.0 https://commons.wikimedia. org/wiki/File:Morpeth_Castle_August_2017.jpg)

The early sixteenth century saw a brief period when the incumbent Baron Greystoke did occupy it as his residence. Indeed, Margaret, the Dowager Queen of Scotland was entertained by him here in 1515–16, but by the end of this century the castle had fallen into disrepair.

However, the greatest historical event to seek out Morpeth Castle was still to come. During the Civil War, when the castle was owned by the Howard family, a 500-strong Parliamentary garrison managed, despite the poor condition of the building, to hold out for twenty days against a Scottish army said to be almost 3,000 in number, despite the Scots bombarding the castle with six cannon. When the garrison did eventually surrender, the Scots were so impressed by their courage that they allowed them to march out honourably; it was discovered they had suffered only twenty-three casualties as opposed to almost 200 of the Scots.

After the tumult of the Civil War the Howards, now Earls of Carlisle, held on to the castle for 200 years but did little to maintain it, viewing it as a useful source of stone for rebuilding in Morpeth. The exception to this was the gatehouse, which remained occupied. By the mid-nineteenth century the Earl of Carlisle made repairs to the gatehouse and installed

Morpeth Castle Gatehouse in Winter (Landmark Trust)

his agent in it. The gatehouse was first sold in 1916, then bought by Morpeth Borough Council thirty years later; for a time it was used as what must have been the most unusual council house in the country. In 1988 the gatehouse had once again fallen into disrepair and the council decided to lease it to the Landmark Trust, who have run it as a holiday let since 1991.

The castle sits just to the south of Morpeth on a hill with wonderful views over both the quaint town and the magnificent Carlisle Park.

Contact Details:
For bookings: https://www.landmarktrust.org.uk/search-and-book/properties/ morpeth-castle-9482
Or, for queries:
The Landmark Trust, Shottesbrooke, Maidenhead, Berkshire, SL6 3SW.

Swinburne Castle B&B

In the tiny hamlet of Great Swinburne the first real mention of the place is when King Henry I granted the Hadston barony to the oddly-named Ankstel de Wirecestre, but by the mid-twelfth century it was the property of two equally oddly-named brothers, Radulf and Pagan, and the barony had been split in two with Pagan being the owner of Great Swinburne. His son John changed his surname to Swinburne, had three sons and enlarged his landowning portfolio by acquiring Chollerton. The eldest son, Nicholas, duly inherited Great Swinburne but here the line ended when his marriage produced only daughters. His eldest daughter, Juliana, married Gilbert de Middleton in 1279 and the couple had two sons. Gilbert inherited his father's more extensive estates in 1310 and handed Great Swinburne over to his younger brother John, but he was master of Great Swinburne for only eight years as he chose to join his brother in the Mitford Gang, which terrorised Northumberland until 1318 when the two Middleton brothers were executed.

The crown took over Great Swinburne but found that, with the shortage of money in Northumberland at the time and the threat of war, it was impossible to sell and the property was instead let on a series of short term leases. This situation persisted until the estate was finally purchased by Roger Widdrington. The manor house which was at Great Swinburne did not satisfy the ambitious and security-conscious Roger, so he knocked it down and in 1346 built a fortified tower on the site instead and named it Swinburne Castle. Just three years after this, Roger became head of the Widdrington family after his brother died without issue and Swinburne Castle became the home for a cadet branch of the family. The tower certainly seems to have been strong and well-maintained as it appears in the surveys of the border made in 1415 and 1541.

The leadership of the Widdrington family changed again in 1592–93 when Sir Henry Widdrington died without producing heirs and the seniority passed to Edward of Great Swinburne. Edward did not live long to enjoy it and by 1592 his eldest son, Henry, had inherited. By 1596 Great Swinburne had achieved some small importance because Henry was Deputy Warden of the Middle March. It was in this year that Sir Robert Kerr of Cessford successfully rode his raid on Great Swinburne to rescue a captured reiver. In doing so he took Roger Widdrington, Henry's younger brother, prisoner. Henry went on to enjoy a successful life being knighted in 1603 and then elected to parliament a year later as MP for Northumberland. Following a term as High Sheriff of Northumberland in 1606 he was re-elected to parliament in 1614 and 1621. He married Mary Curwen, the daughter of Sir Henry Curwen (who served as High Sheriff of Cumberland and as MP for the county).

After Sir Henry's death in 1623, his eldest son, William, inherited at the age of just 13, before becoming head of the family upon reaching maturity. He was knighted at the age of 22 in 1632, and married Mary Thorold six years later. He went on to be elected to parliament in 1640 and served in both the short and long parliaments. In the same year he oversaw the construction of a new manor house which was built next to the now ruinous old tower. These were turbulent times with the Civil War breaking out two years later. Sir William was a supporter of King Charles I and was expelled from parliament as a result. Taking to the battlefield, Sir William fought in battles in Yorkshire and Lincolnshire and was rewarded by being made the 1st Baronet Widdrington of Widdrington in July 1642. In the following year he served as governor of Lincoln and was elevated to the peerage after being made the 1st Baron Widdrington of Blankney (the property of his father-in-law). In 1644 he played a part in the defence of York and after Charles's defeat at Marston Moor was forced to flee with the Duke of Newcastle into exile in Hamburg. Four years later parliament condemned him to death (in his absence) and ordered the confiscation of his estates. In 1650 he returned to Scotland at the side of King Charles II and a year later he was mortally wounded during the Battle of Wigan.

Sir William was succeeded by his son, who was named after his father. This new Sir William became a colonel in the Regiment of Foot Guards in 1660 and was governor of Berwick from 1660 until his death in 1675. His son, the 3rd Baron William Widdrington of Blankney, found that the burden of running so large an estate was too much for the family finances and he sold Great Swinburne to successful Newcastle merchant Thomas Riddell in 1678, thus bringing to an end over 300 years association with the estate.

The Riddells remained there until this century when the property was sold to Dick and Zoe Murphy. One of the Riddell owners decided that the manor house was no longer suitable and around 1760 he oversaw the building of another, grander house. To do so he knocked down the old tower (leaving the two vaults) and the earlier house became servants' quarters and stabling. This mansion lasted only until 1980s, when it was in turn demolished along with the two vaults and remaining relics of the old tower. There is still much to see, however, with parts of the remaining house being over 300 years old.

The house is set in beautiful parkland and gardens. There are many enchanting walks, and part of the house is now given over to a Bed and Breakfast, the bedrooms of which have spectacular southerly views over Hadrian's Wall. The owners pride themselves on the warm welcome they extend to every guest and breakfast features local produce and home-laid eggs. There is also a tennis court and, in addition to the many fine walks, the area is superb for cycling. Furthermore the house is ideally situated for touring other historic Northumbrian locations including Hadrian's Wall and Wallington Hall. The Barrasford Arms is a marvellous pub and restaurant and lies only half an hour's walk from the house, while the attractive market town of Hexham is just 10 miles away and the boutique Roman village of

Corbridge just 6 miles. The house lies only 2 miles from the River Tyne and is an ideal base for those wishing an angling break.

Further details:
https://www.sawdays.co.uk/britain/england/northumberland/swinburne-
    castle/

Facilities
The house is relatively remote and a car is a must.

Battle of Hedgeley Moor

Just north of the small picturesque villages of Powburn and Glanton lies Hedgeley Moor. It was here on 25 April 1664 that a 6,000-strong Yorkist force under Lord Montagu clashed with a similarly sized Lancastrian force under the Duke of Somerset. The commander of the Lancastrian force had set his men up to stop the Yorkists from reaching Scotland where they were to negotiate an extension to a truce. Among the Lancastrian force were the Northumbrians Sir Ralph Percy and Sir Ralph Grey, and other Lancastrians, Lord Roos and Lord Hungerford.

The battle was a relatively uncomplicated one which began with an exchange of archery. Following this, Montagu advanced his army northwards across the moor, but as they approached the Lancastrian army the left flank, consisting of 2,000 men under Lord Roos and Lord Hungerford, broke unexpectedly and fled the field leaving their allies facing a much larger force. Lord Montague paused to reorganise his force before advancing to make contact with the now depleted enemy. The Lancastrians were quickly pushed back by weight of numbers and many of them fled the field at this point. Sir Ralph Percy and his retainers remained behind in a courageous, but futile, last stand. Quickly overwhelmed, Sir Ralph and his men were cut down with Percy reputed to have uttered as he died the enigmatic phrase: 'I have saved the bird in my bosom.'

Directions
The site of the battle is on the east side of the A697 approximately 2 miles
    north of Powburn. A lay-by opposite a woodyard allows cars to park and

pedestrians can then enter the area that was the centre of the battlefield where there are stones and an information board. Among these is a square sandstone pillar known as Percy's Cross.

The Border Reivers

The final kick of the first stage of the wars of independence came during the closing years of the fifteenth century. In 1496 the Scottish King James IV decided to support the claim of the pretender to the English crown, Perkin Warbeck. James invaded Northumberland and began a brutal campaign which saw several tower houses thrown down and destroyed amid mass slaughter. Warbeck was so disgusted by the brutality that he withdrew, and the failure of King James to take Norham Castle allowed the English to regroup. Under the leadership of Thomas Howard, Earl of Surrey, the war was carried into Scotland, but the earl refused to meet James in single combat to decide the future of Berwick. By 1499 a peace treaty, the Treaty of Stirling, restored peace between the two kingdoms culminating with the marriage of James to Henry's eldest daughter.

By the beginning of the sixteenth century the two nations were officially at peace, but for the people of Northumberland (and the other border counties) the continual wars had hardened the character and left many families without money or enough workable land to make living comfortable or even, in many cases, possible. As a result of this constant warfare, the upland clans of the Charltons, Halls, Milburns, Robsons, etc, from places such as Tynedale, Redesdale and, to a lesser extent, Coquetdale, had developed a warlike nature which depended on raiding. In an extension to the events of the Mitford Gang of the fourteenth century, these so-called 'Border Reivers' did not limit their depredations to cross-border raiding, but were by no means averse to taking from their neighbouring Northumbrians and Cumbrians.

A system of wardens was put in place and border laws were established, but the strife continued largely unabated. King James remained discontented with what he perceived as his poorer position compared to his southerly neighbour, and initial good relations with King Henry VIII gave way to annoyance and a decline in relations between the two monarchs. By 1510, King James was looking for any excuse to take exception to the English and their king.

One minor event which gave him something else to hold against the English occurred when a truce day was held in 1511. Truce days were an established part of border law and were the coming together of English and Scottish border officers, often wardens, to hear and settle cases under their jurisdiction. The Scottish warden Sir Robert Ker had a reputation as being a harsh enforcer of these laws (although the Kers were rampant reivers themselves). This alone made him a target for many of the Northumbrian reivers and at the truce day he was attacked, contrary to the terms of truce days, and murdered by three Englishmen. The three, John 'the Bastard' Heron, Lilburn and Starhead, had obviously conspired against the warden and they enacted their cold-blooded scheme with alacrity.

John Heron was widely known as the 'Bastard of Ford', as he was the illegitimate son of Heron of Ford. He was an extremely colourful character and an undoubted hardcase. The murder of Ker (some English claimed it came in a duel, but this is unlikely) became a national incident and soured relations further between the two monarchs. Some sources report that Heron and Lilburn were delivered up for justice and died in captivity in Fast Castle, but this is incorrect. Lilburn did indeed suffer this fate while the other collaborator, Starhead, was murdered by Scots far south of the frontier and his head subsequently displayed in Edinburgh on the order of King James. John the Bastard survived, however, and it is said he fought at the Battle of Flodden in 1513. It is known that he was awarded a royal pension for his activities (possibly during the battle) and that he died, while still relatively young, in 1524.

Shortly after this Sir Andrew Barton, a Scottish pirate and favourite of King James, was killed by the English and this provided further excuse for bad feeling. This culminated in the renewal of Scotland's alliance with France (which was at war with Italy) and finally resulted in King James agreeing to the French King Louis' request that he invade England to provide a distraction in 1513. This invasion in turn led to the Battle of Flodden, at which the Scottish suffered their worst defeat and King James and much of his leading nobility were slain.

The Northumbrian borderers played a leading role at Flodden under the command of Lord Dacre. His Lordship may have proven his worth during the battle – indeed, it could be argued he saved the day, but he found it rather harder to control the English riding clans in his role as warden. Dacre was particularly irked by the ferocious plundering of the clans of Redesdale and North Tynedale, many of whom had ridden with him at Flodden, and he became embroiled in Scottish politics just two years after Flodden when he welcomed Queen Margaret of Scotland and her new husband, the Earl of Angus, at his headquarters at Harbottle Castle in Upper Coquetdale.

The post of warden was no sinecure; there was constant raid and counter-raid during the years after Flodden. In 1521 the garrison of Harbottle Castle rescued a large number of cattle which had been stolen by Scottish reivers, but on the same night the English warden suffered a reverse when an estimated 500 masked reivers from Teviotdale burned the village of Learmouth.

Throughout the sixteenth century and into the first decade of the seventeenth, the border reivers formed a gang system of closely interwoven clan and extended family groups, largely through their habit of intermarriage, often across the border line despite laws to the contrary. The reivers were highly-skilled light cavalry, especially over rough terrain which they knew exceptionally well; they could travel lengthy distances at night or day without being observed, and could plan their forays using military precision and skill. In the spring of 1596 a prominent reiver (who had been illegally captured on a truce day), Kinmont Willie Armstrong, was being held in Carlisle Castle in Cumbria, but Sir Walter Scott of Buccleuch, Keeper of Liddesdale and prominent border heidsman (the leader of a clan or important branch – or sept – of a clan) and noble, had promised to free him. After he failed to do so legally, Buccleuch ran a very well planned and highly efficient raid on the massive castle and managed to successfully rescue Kinmont Willie. The rescue quickly attracted a mixture of approbation, praise and admiration for Buccleuch.

The praise reserved for Buccleuch seems to have stung his brother-in-law, Sir Robert Kerr of Cessford. Robert was the heidsman of the powerful and influential Cessford branch of the Kerrs and Warden of the Scottish Middle March. Despite this, Kerr was a notorious reiver himself and had committed a number of murders, many of them during family feuds. Kerr was undoubtedly angered by, and jealous of, the praise given to his subordinate, the two cordially disliked each other. Just four months after the Carlisle raid, Kerr sensed an opportunity to prove that he was equal to anything Buccleuch could do. A reiver named James Young of the Cove had been taken prisoner by the Northumbrian Selby family and was being held at Swinburn Castle, which was the property of the Widdrington Deputy Warden of the English Middle March, and Kerr tried a variety of legal means to secure his freedom. When these failed he determined to do as Buccleuch had, and began to plan an audacious foray deep into Tynedale.

Cessford and his handpicked men were faced with a 42-mile journey made at night through hostile country held by the notorious Tynedale and Redesdale clans, including the Robsons, followed by the task of breaking into Swinburne and getting back across the border with Young. It seems likely that Cessford also followed Buccleuch in securing allies among the English borderers, because running such a foray with a relatively small force would have been almost impossible without help. No doubt he exploited the extensive family ties that reached across the border along with the links between 'professional' reivers.

In any event, on the night of 27 August, Cessford led his foray and successfully rescued Young. He did it without bloodshed, but this is unsurprising because on this occasion he was not there for bloodshed, and fighting would probably have been disastrous for the foray. Cessford did, however, take a number of captives, including Roger Widdrington, the brother of the deputy warden.

Clearly pleased with his night's work Cessford, who was nothing if not a dashing killer, wrote to his opposite number outlining the reasons he had run the illegal foray to free Young. Furthermore, the English warden, Sir Ralph Eure, seems to have been keen to accept his reasons and, probably in an effort to deflect criticism from himself, blamed Widdrington for having held Young illegally as part of an ongoing feud with Cessford. The raid resulted in Widdrington resigning his position after Eure forbade him from pursuing his vendetta with Cessford, only for Eure himself to resign shortly afterwards and for the incoming warden, Sir Robert Carey, who cordially despised Cessford, re-appointed Widdrington.

For Cessford the events of 27 August were a mere prelude to a series of bloody attacks carried out in pursuit of his feuds. Several Selbys were murdered by Kerr or his men in the next few months. Cessford and his gang of ruffians attacked a number of communities and towers during this time including Weetwood Tower, Downham, and Branxton. The people of Mindrum wisely saw what was coming and promptly paid blackmail to Cessford to avoid his predations. Cessford claimed that his feud with the Selbys had arisen after the murder of his cousin, John Dalgliesh, but English intelligence sources firmly believed it had come about after the Selbys had killed Ralph 'Shortneck' Burn and captured Geordie Burn (who was subsequently hanged by Carey) during a 'hot trod' (a legally approved pursuit foray made to apprehend reivers who had recently struck). It would seem that the Burns had been under the protection of Cessford.

It would seem that Sir Robert Kerr of Cessford pursued multiple feuds with a variety of Northumbrian families and clans during this period. The most famous of these feuds was a longstanding one with the Charltons of Tynedale. The Charltons had been behind his grandfather's murder and had kept his sword as a souvenir. At the same time, Cessford was in feud with the Storeys around Wooler. This feud had arisen after Kerr's men had ridden a foray on the lands of a man named only as the laird Baggot, and when he had ridden hot trod in pursuit, the reivers had turned the tables on their pursuers and murdered Baggot and two other men. In response, the Storeys vowed revenge for the murder of Baggot (who was related to them by marriage) and killed Cessford's shepherd. As a result, Kerr swore that he would have his vengeance upon the Storey clan and duly mounted a number of murderous forays against them. (Those interested in a more detailed account of the bloody Northumbrian adventures of Kerr of Cessford and his rivalry with Sir Robert Carey should read Fraser, George MacDonald, *The Steel Bonnets: The Story of the Anglo-Scottish Border Reivers* (HarperCollins, 2012), also see Tait, Jon, *Dick the Devil's Bairns. Breaking the Border Mafia* (Tredition, 2018).

The Battle of Flodden

By 1513 it seemed that the whole of Western Europe was becoming involved in war. France was campaigning in Italy, and England and the Holy Roman Empire had allied together and were, in turn, threatening an invasion of France. King Louis, anxious of this threat of a war on two fronts but unwilling to withdraw from Italy, re-made the auld alliance with Scotland and requested that King James invade England to ensure that the English army did not invade France. In return he promised to make James king of England as well as Scotland upon their victory, and to mount a crusade with him at a later date.

James, impressionable, passionate and eager to prove himself after what he saw as a series of humiliations at the hands of the English King Henry VIII, agreed. In what was akin to a war fever, the people of Scotland rallied round their young king and an army of at least 30,000 men was assembled, the greatest that Scotland had ever put into the field. The Scottish borderers, under the command of Lord Hume, were assembled earliest and, anxious to give vent to their aggression, they mounted a large raid on Northumberland. Burning several villages and carrying off a large amount of booty, the force was retreating when they were ambushed not far from the site of the 1402 Battle of Homildon Hill. The Scots were routed and although Hume escaped, he left behind 500 of his men dead and 400 more as prisoners of the English. This escapade, which should perhaps have given the Scots pause, gained the name the 'Ill Raid'.

James and his army crossed into England on 22 August, but there was already some anxiety. His force, made up of men from all over Scotland, was fairly inexperienced and they had just been re-armed with, and trained in the use of, the long continental spear. This weapon had gained great success on the Continent, but was perhaps not the best weapon for the terrain in which the Scots would have to fight. The force also contained a number of artillery pieces which were heavy and unwieldy, having to be drawn by teams of oxen. They were commanded by a master gunner, but crewed by largely inexperienced men.

For all this, the invasion started well for the Scots as they managed to capture the castles at Norham, Wark, Etal and Ford. However, the army had suffered losses in the capture of Norham and there had already been a spate of desertions as men became dispirited by the losses, the extremely poor weather, and the disease which began to spread through the Scottish camp.

That wily old campaigner the Earl of Surrey (Thomas Howard, 2nd Duke of Norfolk) ordered all possible forces to muster at Newcastle, and by 4 September had assembled a force estimated to number 26,000.

The vast majority of the men were billmen and archers, with the only cavalry being a detachment of 1,500 light horsemen, mainly drawn from the reiving clans, from the Borders under the command of Lord Dacre. As the English army marched northwards, Surrey experienced supply shortages and realised that he would have to bring the campaign to a swift conclusion. He therefore sent his herald to challenge King James to battle on 9 September. King James, no doubt angered by some of the barbed words of the challenge, accepted but when Surrey entered the Till valley it became obvious that James had chosen a site which, in Surrey's words, was more like a fortress and he suggested that they descend to give battle on the plain of Milfield. James declined this offer and Surrey then took a very risky chance by moving his army off to encircle the Scottish position to the north so as to stand between the enemy and his homeland. The Scots failed to take advantage of this opportunity to attack and instead repositioned their army. This resulted in his artillery being badly positioned and the English were able to form up on Piper's Hill although they were still below their enemies on Branxton Hill.

Flodden would prove to be a battle decided by technology as much as by the courage and steadfastness of the participants. The English army which fought at Flodden still largely eschewed several modern developments and the longbowman still played an important role, although the archers were a different proposal from their thirteenth-century origins. As they had proven in recent conflicts, most notably at Agincourt, they were no longer as vulnerable as they had been in the

English Bill from Arncliffe, N. Yorks, claimed to have been used at Flodden (Monstrelet / CC-BY-SA-3.0)

past and could act as light infantrymen when the opportunity arose. The English also eschewed the use of the long pike and had instead adapted the traditional 8ft bill, making it into a weapon which combined cutting and stabbing blades into a very effective close-combat weapon.

The armies arrayed themselves for the clash. On the English side the men were bolstered by the flying of the Red Dragon of England (indicating no quarter) and the men of Durham by the much-revered red velvet Banner of St Cuthbert. Surrey arrayed his force into three main formations. On the right Surrey himself commanded, in the centre was his eldest son the Lord Admiral, and on the left another son, Edmund. Behind the main line, as a mobile reserve, were the majority of Border light horsemen under Dacre, while the force under Sir Edward Stanley had become detached from the main force and appeared on the right flank later in the battle. The Scots arrayed themselves into a matching formation with their right commanded by the king, the centre under the earls of Crawford, Errol and Montrose, while the left was under Lord Hume and Earl Huntly.

The battle opened at approximately 4 pm with an artillery duel in which the Scots came off decidedly the worse. Their own artillery could not be depressed enough to fire on the English army while the English, with experienced gunners and lighter artillery, were able to catch the Scots in a crossfire. It was obvious to James that this situation could not be maintained, but he was fearful of ordering his army to retreat back over the ridge so that it was out of sight of the English artillery.

James, no doubt angered and disappointed at the failure of his much-vaunted artillery, instead ordered the attack. It has been said that the advance took place largely, and surprisingly, in silence. It was the mass of men, mainly borderers, under Hume and Huntly on the left who advanced first and most quickly. The slope they faced was not as steep or treacherous as that facing the others and they were able to advance steadily, remembering the lessons they had been given in the use of the pike. The remaining battles of the Scottish army followed. On the left, the battle of Hume and Huntly, consisting of a mix of Border pikemen and Gordon clansmen, came under fire from the English archers as well as the artillery. For once, however, the longbow fire was largely ineffective here with this subsequently being blamed on the poor weather, but a definite contributing factor was that many of the Scots had also been equipped with large wooden shields known as pavishes. Despite suffering some casualties, Hume's battle was still in good order when it reached the English lines and the battle of Edmund Howard.

At this point it seemed that James's faith in the continental pike had been well placed; the Scots forced the English back, with many turning to flee and being pursued by Gordon clansmen. Although much of his battle had disintegrated, Edmund Howard fought on. He was knocked to the floor on no less than three occasions and his standard bearer was cut down.

The situation for the English was dire. The jubilant battle of Lord Hume could now turn the flank of the Lord Admiral and possibly win the day, but it was here that Dacre and his often maligned border horsemen proved themselves. Dacre and his men spurred themselves into the position abandoned by the men of Edmund Howard's battle and met their fellow borderers, who appeared, in the heat of victory, to have loosened their formation. Others still found the actions of both English and Scottish borderers on that bloody day to be perfidious. It was claimed that Hume and his borderers made no attempt to turn the English flank, and that when the borderers met in battle they made only a show of a fierce clash.

It might have been, however, that Hume, with his eye for a battle's direction, had seen something which prevented him from ordering his men to turn against the Lord Admiral. The rest of the Scottish army had run into trouble before it had even encountered the English. The soaked surface proved extremely slippery, but then they encountered what proved to be a deep, water-filled and marshy ditch, which held up the advance and made a shambles of the vital pike formations. Training and discipline was forgotten, but the Scots bravely hauled themselves up the slope towards the English who awaited them, bills at the ready.

At first the ferocity of the Scots attack pushed the men of the Lord Admiral back. The battle of the Lord Admiral, however, did not break, and instead slowed and then halted the Scottish advance of the men under Crawford, Errol and Montrose. Behind them came King James and his great battle, made up largely of the nobility and clergy of the realm, but they were once again held up, this time by Surrey's battle. The king, frustrated at the lack of progress, certainly proved his courage if not his wisdom. He fought from the front as a 'mean soldier', and it was even rumoured that he hefted a pike alongside the rank and file of his army.

Surrey's tactics now came to the fore as the longer English battles began to outflank the Scots. At this point, Scots casualties began to mount as the English billmen were able to get within their ranks and within reach of the 18ft-long pikes. The English quickly found that their bills could in fact slash off the ash shafts of the pikes, rendering them useless. Many Scots, seeing the failing in these new and largely untrusted weapons, quickly abandoned them and instead drew their swords, but to little avail.

The fighting was ferocious with little or no quarter given, but after three or four hours, the Scots broke. Many of the nobles and knights were down by this stage and those common men left to the rear of the formations no doubt saw little point to remaining; many began to melt away to seek a way home through dangerous, enemy countryside. At this point the English archers returned to the fray, helping to hack down embattled Scots, or picking off prominent Scots with their arrows. Realising that the battle was lost, those Scots who remained in the fray grimly resolved to sell their lives as dearly as possible.

King James was among them. Even now, however, he sought victory. Surrounded by a band of protective retainers the king attempted to charge at Surrey himself in the hope that cutting down the commander of the English host might prove decisive. The king very nearly reached him, but under the increasing English onslaught he fell, unseen, cut down by the numerous English bills.

The Earls of Argyll and Lennox remained in their positions on Branxton Hill with up to 6,000 highlanders, even though it was clear that their king was endangered. It has been reported that, as the lightest armoured and least disciplined of the Scottish forces, they had been ordered to remain to guard the artillery. At this point, the battle led by Stanley belatedly reached the battlefield. They launched a devastating longbow volley against the lightly-clad highlanders before advancing against them. The majority fled as soon as they were confronted by the billmen, although the two earls remained behind to fight and be slain.

The remaining Scots were now in full retreat. Some did allege that there was a rout or pursuit, but there is little evidence for this; the final state of

Flodden Cross and Field (© drhfoto/Adobe Stock)

the battle was too confused, although it is possible that some elements of the English army, including no doubt many of the Northumbrian cavalry, did pursue some of the Scots for a short distance. Back on the bloody field, the shrieks and moans of dying men echoed as men prowled the field seeking booty. The Battle of Flodden was over.

Surrey and many of his men, however, were left unsure over the result of the battle. The poor weather and darkening sky meant that they were unable to discern whether there were any Scots left on the field and so the majority of the English remained standing at arms throughout the night. At first light the Lord Hume and several hundred border horsemen made an audacious attempt to recover the valuable Scottish artillery, but they were easily defeated and fled the field once again.

The increasing light showed Surrey just how complete his victory had been. The field would have been a shocking and horrid sight as thousands of bodies were strewn about, many of them having been stripped naked by scavengers. No one knows the true extent of the slaughter, but historians put the Scottish death toll at anywhere between 7,000 and 17,000, with most contemporary historians agreeing a figure of at least 8,000. Among them was the badly mutilated and partially stripped body of King James.

The royal corpse was found by none other than Lord Dacre, who had known the king previously. Joining their sovereign in death was the cream of Scottish nobility including ten earls (Argyll, Bothwell, Cassilis, Caithness, Crawford, Errol, Lennox, Morton, Montrose and Rothes), nine Lords of Parliament (Lords Avondale, Borthwick, Elphinstone, Innermeath, Maxwell, Ross, Seton, Semphill and Erskine), and at least twenty-four notable chieftains, nobles and knights. In addition, five prominent members of the clergy also fell, including James's natural son, Alexander Stewart, Archbishop of St Andrews and Lord Chancellor of Scotland (he was joined by the Bishop of the Isles, the Abbot of Kilwinning, the Abbot Inchaffray, and the Prior of Torpichen Preceptory and Lord High Treasurer of Scotland). English casualties were placed at approximately 1,500, the majority of them coming from the battle of Edmund Howard.

Following the conclusion of the battle, it is said that the borderers returned to their normal ways, with the Scottish borderers pillaging their own baggage train while the English borderers also pillaged the English supplies.

In the aftermath of the battle, Lord Dacre escorted the bloodied and mutilated body of King James IV, who had been excommunicated after his invasion, to Berwick, where it was shown to two captured Scottish courtiers, including James' sergeant-porter, who confirmed that it was indeed the king. It was then transported to Sheen Priory near London via Newcastle and York. Meanwhile, the captured booty, including hundreds of suits of armour, was auctioned off on the battlefield and, demonstrating the scale of the battle, the list of horses which had been taken ran to twenty-four pages. The news of King James's death travelled far and wide. The torn and bloodstained surcoat of the king were taken to the English queen, Catherine of Aragon, at Woburn Abbey, and she dispatched them to her husband, Henry VIII, in France as proof. For the shattered Scots, the loss of so many nobles and the king was a huge shock, and rumours and conspiracy theories sprang up quickly.

James's embalmed body lay at Sheen for many years, despite King Henry having been given papal dispensation to have it buried in consecrated ground at St Pauls. The corpse was subsequently lost when the priory was demolished during the reformation and rumour and legend took over its fate. There were claims that the king had survived, or had been killed retreating from the field, and when a well at Hume Castle was being cleared in the eighteenth century, there were even claims that a skeleton wearing a chain around its waist (a symbol of kinghood) was discovered in a side passage and secretly re-interred at Holyrood Abbey, while other legends from a century earlier claim that these events took place at Roxburgh Castle or at Berry Moss near Kelso.

The Battle of Flodden (or, as it perhaps should have been called the Battle of Branxton Hill) was the worst disaster to befall the Scottish nation. Not only had Scotland lost her revered king – he became the last British king to be killed in battle – she had also lost almost an entire generation of her leading nobility and it was said that there was not a family untouched by the catastrophe.

A car-park is situated just off the road. There is a fairly steep walk up to the memorial cross but it is certainly worth it. There is no access charge. There are numerous information boards around the battle site which explain the disposition of forces, etc. There is also a largely comfortable circular walk around the site.

Flodden Monument (© drhfoto/Adobe Stock)

Preston Tower

Preston Tower stands near the village of Chathill in the north of Northumberland between Alnwick and Berwick-upon-Tweed. Built between 1392 and 1399, the tower is a rather grand version of the pele towers which minor members of the nobility and landowners constructed during the many years of border strife between England and Scotland. In the time of the Battle of Agincourt in 1415 there were almost eighty such towers in Northumberland. The builder of Preston tower was a Sir Robert Harbottle. Sir Robert would have been enmeshed within Northumbrian and, quite possibly, national politics, and would probably have known Henry 'Hotspur' Percy extremely well, as the two would have been squires together in France and would have had other social contact.

The first official mention of him is his indictment for a murder which he allegedly committed in 1392 while acting in the service of the Constable of Berwick. It seems his defence was successful as he was subsequently pardoned. At this time Preston was a township in the Embleton Barony which was the property of John of Gaunt, Duke of Lancaster. An extremely influential man who acted as de facto regent during the minority of Richard II, his ownership of Embleton and, with it, Preston, meant that Harbottle was a vassal of this powerful nobleman. The duke took a great interest in his northern lands, fortifying Dunstanburgh Castle and probably encouraging, perhaps even aiding, Sir Robert to complete his tower.

When the Duke of Lancaster died in 1399, the same year Preston Tower was completed, his son, Henry Bolingbroke, who had been banished by Richard II, returned to regain his lands and titles and, with the help of the Percys, he overthrew Richard and became King Henry IV. Thus, just as Preston Tower was completed, the barony of which it was a part became crown land.

The year 1399 was undoubtedly a big year for Sir Robert. He may have marched with the Percys, including Hotspur, to meet with Henry Bolingbroke, and he may have aided in the efforts to overthrow King Richard II, but this is speculation. We do know for certain that in 1399 Sir Robert married the daughter and heiress of Breton knight, Sir Bertram Monboucher of Horton Tower, near Blyth.

Sir Robert died in 1419 and was succeeded by his son, another Sir Robert. This Sir Robert Harbottle had married a daughter of Sir Robert Ogle in 1417, and the wedding contained a rather unusual instruction which resulted in Sir Robert and his new wife living with Sir Robert Ogle at his home for a period of two years. The couple did, however, gain an estate at Newstead as part of the dowry. This Sir Robert seems to have been quite influential as he was appointed as sheriff in 1439, a post he held until his death in 1443.

Sir Robert was succeeded by his son John. It was this man who undertook some repairs to the tower, although he seems to have been somewhat cash-strapped because he replaced the roof with thatch rather than the more expensive lead or stone, despite the risk of fire. John's son was named Ralph and his marriage clearly reflected the continued links with the powerful and influential Northumberland elite. His bride was none other than Margaret, daughter of Sir Ralph Percy (who was killed at the Battle of Hedgeley Moor in 1446), and the two had a son whom they named Guiscard.

By the sixteenth century, border skirmishes and raiding, even when the two nations were officially at peace, was commonplace with clans of Border Reivers raiding not only across the border, but also on their own side of it. The pele towers such as Preston became refuges not only for the landowners, but also for the nearby communities, and provided some security against the almost constant raiding.

At the time of the Battle of Flodden (1513) the owner of the tower was Sir Guiscard Harbottle. Sir Guiscard was a part of the English army which fought at Flodden and he was among the 1,500 Englishmen killed in the decisive English victory. Sir Guiscard was said to have been slain in hand-to-hand combat with King James IV. Guiscard left behind two young children, a boy and a girl. The boy died while in his teens and so the estate passed down to his daughter, Eleanor, commonly known as Lenna. She married Sir Thomas Percy and when he became the 7th Earl of Northumberland in 1557, Preston became part of the Northumberland estate. Throughout the rest of the sixteenth century, while nobles and landowners in the south of England built luxurious country manors, those in Northumberland continued to be most concerned with defence and security when building their own homes.

Unfortunately, Earl Thomas was executed for his role in the rising of the northern earls in 1572 and his estates and property were confiscated, although a cadet branch of the Harbottle family managed to convince Queen Elizabeth I to rent Preston to them. This arrangement lasted for almost a century.

In the 1950s the renowned architectural historian Sir Nikolaus Pevsner stated that Preston Tower was among the most spectacular pieces of medieval masonry in England, with the huge stone blocks used in the construction of its 7ft thick walls bearing the same masons' marks as those found down the coast at Warkworth Castle.

The era of the Border Reivers came to an end with the union of the crowns in 1603 as many of the border clansmen were outlawed and, without the border to shelter behind, hunted down and either executed or banished from the country. Following this, the owners of Preston Tower decided that defence was no longer such a necessity and that they could afford to economise. They thus had half of the tower demolished, leaving the remains seen today, and the stone used for the construction of farm buildings on their estate.

In 1663 the estate was sold to William Armorer of Ellington and then it passed through the hands of Sir Thomas Wood of Barton and Edward Craster before the Baker-Cresswell family bought the property in 1861 and they have possessed it ever since.

A tour of the tower is very rewarding. The ground floor includes a guard room and prison, while the first floor, consisting of a bedroom and living room, have been decorated and furnished in the way they might have been during the fifteenth and sixteenth centuries. The second floor of the tower features an extensive display commemorating the Battle of Flodden, along with interesting displays of artefacts and accounts from Border history and from the esteemed Border Ballads. Also of interest on the second floor is the clock mechanism. The huge clock was installed in 1864 and uses a mechanism which is very similar to that which drives Big Ben in London. The clock strikes the hour on a bell which weighs approximately 500 kg and is housed in one of the towers. Visitors can also visit the top of the tower, from where there are spectacular views over the Northumbrian countryside.

The house is also worth a visit and in pleasant weather the grounds are a very lovely setting. There are three short walks for visitors and the gardens are a delight to those who enjoy unusual plants, trees and shrubs. These include such rarities as tulip trees, a Gingko Biloba, and the umbrella shaped cockspur thorn (a North American hawthorn with 2in thorns) which stands near the car park. A woodland walk provides seclusion and takes visitors through beautiful beech woodland, which provides a home for the Red Squirrel, to a lovely secluded spring which is used to provide water for the house via a tank in the tower.

Holidaymakers who wish to stop in the grounds of Preston Tower and use the location as a base to explore this part of Northumberland can stay in the self-catering Tower Cottage. This is a spacious, single-bedroom, cottage which is available for rent on a weekly basis. Facilities for guests include free access to the tower and grounds and a hard surface tennis court. Interested parties should contact Mike Chambers at Northumbria Coast and Country Cottages on 01665 830 783 or at n c c c . m i k e c h a m b e r s @ btinternet.com.

Preston Tower (mattbuck / CC BY-SA 4.0)

Directions

Car – Preston Tower is signposted from the only dual-carriageway section of the A1 between Alnwick and Berwick. Turn off the A1 7¼ miles north of Alnwick (northbound) or 7¼ miles south of Belford (southbound). Follow the road for approximately 2 miles until you reach a second sign for Preston Tower.

Opening Times

The pele tower and garden walks are open every day of the year, 10 am – 6 pm.

Admission Charges

Adults: £2
Children: £0.50
Concessions & Groups: £1.50

Facilities

Free parking and public toilets are available.

CHAPTER 4

The Civil War

The events now known as the English Civil War were a complex series of conflicts between 1637 and 1651, and involved not only England but Scotland and Ireland as well. King Charles I firmly believed that he ruled by the authority of God and that he could impose his royal will and prerogative with absolute authority.

In 1637 Charles attempted to impose ecclesiastical and doctrinal changes on Scotland and this led to a revolution in Scotland with the so-called Covenanters resisting the king. Charles tried on two occasions to raise an army to crush Scottish resistance, but failed because of hostility among many of his English subjects to his autocratic style. In 1640 a Scottish army, which was well led but consisted of inexperienced soldiers, invaded Northumberland. Meeting little resistance, the Scots quickly made for Newcastle with the intention of cutting off much of London's coal supply.

On 27 August the Scots, some 20,000 strong, were emplaced above the village of Newburn (now part of Newcastle) where there was an important ford over the River Tyne, the capture of which would allow them to advance into Newcastle. Lord Conway, the English commander, had only 3,000 men at his command but quickly constructed breastworks to cover the two fords and settled down for the night hoping for reinforcements.

The next morning the Scots, from the higher ground, could clearly see the English dispositions; an artillery bombardment quickly eliminated the English artillery and caused casualties among the few cavalry. It quickly became clear to the English that their position was hopeless and once the Scottish army advanced, the English were routed and fled.

Two days later, Newcastle surrendered to the Scots. There were many Scots living in and around Newcastle and at first the occupiers were welcomed, but this situation soon turned sour. King Charles was forced to recall parliament, which refused to fund his war against the Scots and instead he was forced to pay for the billeting of the Scots in Newcastle until they withdrew in the late summer of 1641.

A year later the situation between Charles and his subjects erupted into conflict. Charles sent the Earl of Newcastle to take command of Newcastle and the Northern Army. This army contained a large number of Northumbrians. In eleven foot regiments raised in Northumberland, there were at least ninety-three Northumbrian officers. Those Northumbrians who raised the eleven foot regiments were Charles Brandling of Alnwick, Sir Robert Clavering, Thomas Forster, Edward Grey, Sir Thomas Haggerston of Haggerston, Ralph Hepburn, Sir John Marley of Newcastle, Sir George Muschamp of Barmoor, Sir Thomas Riddell, Gilbert Swinhoe, and Lord Widdrington. Out of its sixty cavalry regiments no fewer than nine had been raised and were largely officered by Northumbrians. They included regiments raised by Sir Francis Carnaby of Langley, Sir Francis Anderson of Jesmond, Sir Robert Clavering of Callaly, Sir John Fenwick of Wallington, Sir Edward Grey of Chillingham, George Heron of Chipchase, Sir John Marley of Newcastle, Sir Edward Widdrington of Cartington, and Sir William Widdrington of Great Swinburn. Rolls attest to the presence of no fewer than 113 Northumbrian cavalry officers and these are only those who have been positively identified. It is noticeable that several Northumbrians raised multiple regiments of both foot and cavalry, thus showing the fervour among some for the king.

This Northern Army won a great victory at Adwalton Moor in Yorkshire in June 1643 and established a northern base for the Royalist cause. By the end of the year, however, the Parliamentarians had agreed a treaty known as the Solemn League and Covenant with the Scots. By December a large Scottish army, known as the Army of the Covenant, was on the border under the command of Alexander Leslie, Earl of Leven. In January 1644 over 21,000 men crossed the River Tweed at Coldstream and entered Northumberland. They were faced with a force of only 5,000 under the command of Sir Thomas Glemham. He was a competent commander but had no option but to abandon his position at Alnwick and retreat towards Newcastle in the face of such odds. Leslie was determined to capture Newcastle as it was a vital coal port and was the main port for Royalist weapons coming from the Continent.

By 28 January the Scots were at Morpeth. Heavy rain then slowed progress and by the time the Scots had reached Newcastle the main body of the Northern Army had entered the city. Lord Leven ordered Newcastle to surrender on 3 February but this was refused. Glemham had improved the defences around Newcastle and it became clear that a prolonged siege would probably occur. Leven left six regiments to blockade Newcastle and then took his main body to invest Sunderland; by April the Marquis of Newcastle and much of his army had been forced to retreat to Yorkshire. At the start of July the Royalists were defeated at the Battle of Marston Moor and the Scots army returned on 12 August to besiege Newcastle and Tynemouth.

It was clear that the Royalist position in the north was now hopeless, but the Northumbrian Royalists refused to surrender at Newcastle and Tynemouth. Sir John Marley, the Mayor of Newcastle, was determined to hold out and oversee the defences himself. For two months the walls were bombarded and attempts were made to undermine them. The defenders of Newcastle returned fire from the tower of St Andrew's Church. Leven offered terms of surrender twice more but both were rejected by Marley. Leven threatened to destroy the tower of St Andrew's but Marley responded by moving Scottish prisoners into the steeple.

On 14 October Leven offered terms for a third time. He added to his ultimatum that if no surrender was forthcoming by the morning of 19 October, the Scots would assault the town. Marley again refused to surrender and the Scots launched an multi-pronged attack at seven points in the city walls. Leven's assault force consisted of 11,000 men arrayed against just 2,000 defenders. The Royalists were forced to retreat to the castle keep and in the two-hour long fight that followed, 1,000 Scots and 500 English were killed. Days afterwards, the garrison holding Tynemouth Castle and fort surrendered, effectively ending the war in Northumberland.

It was, however, not quite the end as a Royalist revolt erupted in Northumberland, Durham and Scotland in 1648. In Northumberland the Royalists managed to capture Berwick but Cromwell quickly moved north and re-took the town.

With the rule of Cromwell as Lord-Protector and the rise in puritanism, there was a surge in hysteria surrounding the use of witchcraft. In 1649–50 a series of witch trials were held in Newcastle, with twenty-seven out of thirty being found guilty. Fourteen of these unfortunates were executed on the Town Moor, while a man who was accused of being able to turn into a black cat called Vinegar was executed and burned. The witchfinder appointed by Newcastle was a Scotsman named Cuthbert Nicholson, who was paid 20*s* for every witch he found. The thirty women were stripped to the waist and Nicholson pricked them with a pin. If they did not bleed they were decried as witches. It was believed that Nicholson used a retractable pin and he was later executed for trickery having confessed to being responsible for the deaths of 220 women.

CHAPTER 5

Northumbrian Jacobitism

Northumberland had long remained a stronghold of Catholicism and the area was seen as a nest of popery, and combined with this was a strong loyalty to the Stuarts dating back to the Civil War.

The ruling Hanoverian government of King William were very suspicious of treacherous plots hatched by Northumbrian gentry during the latter part of the seventeenth century, and in 1680 there were strong suspicions that Edward Charlton of Hesleyside was a prominent Jacobite conspirator who was frequently visited by Jacobite spies. By the following year it was strongly, and correctly, suspected that there was a plot to organise a Jacobite invasion to land in the north east. Ten years later, in 1691, a small French force landed at Druridge Bay and plundered the village of Widdrington. Plotting for rebellion and invasion continued apace with plans for a landing and uprising of the Northumbrian gentry supported by the colliers of Newcastle, the seizing of Newcastle, followed by a Scottish invasion and French landing, leading to the successful capture of London and the restoration of Stuart rule. In 1697 Sir John Fenwick of Wallington was executed for being the ringleader of a plot to both assassinate King William and to allow a Stuart-led invasion to land at Newcastle. Although the plotting was constant very little was actually done, and it was only after 1710 when the question of the succession to Queen Anne became prominent that the Northumbrian Jacobites began to plot an uprising in earnest.

The leading Northumbrian Jacobite conspirator was James Radcliffe, 3rd Earl of Derwentwater. The earl had very extensive lands in Northumberland and Cumbria and was absolutely loyal to the Stuart cause. William, 4th Baron Widdrington, was also a key adherent to the cause and was a powerful and rich mine-owner. Other important Jacobite sympathisers in Northumberland included the Haggerstons, the Swinburnes of Capheaton and the Erringtons of Beaufront. These prominent Jacobite families were all Catholics but the Stuarts had their Protestant adherents in the county too. They included two of the area's MPs, William Blackett of Newcastle and Thomas Forster of Bamburgh. The latter came from a very old and prominent Northumbrian family but had fallen on hard times financially, only to bailed out by Bishop Crewe. Blackett, on the other hand, was a wealthy Newcastle merchant who had purchased Wallington Hall from the Fenwick family, who were also Jacobites. Forster believed that the Tory community would rally to the cause once the rebellion began, while Blackett believed he could be instrumental in garnering the support of the mercantile classes in Newcastle. These men would be the Northumbrian ringleaders of the Jacobite Rising of 1715.

When the rising began in the autumn of 1715, some seventy-seven Northumbrian gentlemen threw in their lot with the Jacobites. They were joined by a small contingent of over 200 other Northumbrians, mainly servants of those who were leading the rising. The key Northumbrian Jacobites had gone into hiding when arrest warrants were issued for them, but came out when the rebellion was declared. Blackett, however, seems to have been less sure at this point, locked himself away at Wallington and seems to have played no part.

On 6 October the Northumbrian Jacobites openly declared their rebellion and met on Greenriggs Moor between Sweethope Loughs and Redesmouth. Derwentwater was allegedly reluctant to openly rebel and was persuaded by his wife and brother. At Greenrigg they met with Forster and twenty men but were disappointed that there was no sign of Blackett. The party moved across country and were met by further reinforcements in Rothbury where they spent the night, before moving on to Warkworth the next day. They raised the Stuart banner here and proclaimed James III as king. They then moved southwards and camped on Lesbury Moor to await the promised Scottish invasion. The Northumbrian Jacobites were worried, however. Only 300 or so had turned out, whereas they had expected there to be at least 1,000.

The hoped-for Scottish invasion was nowhere near what they had expected, but by November the mixed Scottish and Northumbrian Jacobite army, still only 1,500 strong, was in Lancashire where it hoped to gain further support. This was not forthcoming and after a brief skirmish at Preston they were forced to surrender.

Five of the Northumbrian Jacobite gentry who had come out in rebellion and had been taken prisoner were subsequently executed. Two, Edmund and John Ord of Weetwood, were killed in battle, and three, William Clavering of Errington, George Gibson of Stonecroft, and Edward Swinburne of Capheaton, died in captivity. The five who were executed were the Earl of Derwentwater, John Hunter, John Shafto of Thockrington, John 'Mad Jack' Hall of Otterburn, and George Collingwood of Eslington. Widdrington was very fortunate to be pardoned while Forster was most likely going to be executed, but escaped thanks to his sister and fled to France.

Wallington Hall

The Fenwick family had long-held a pele tower in the picturesque surroundings of Wallington, but in 1688 Sir William Blackett, a prominent and wealthy Newcastle merchant and shipping magnate, bought the estate from his friends the Fenwicks; both families were Jacobite sympathisers and had a love of ostentatious parties. He immediately knocked down the tower and set about overseeing the construction of what was a glorified shooting lodge. Sir William died in 1705, but the family reputation for partying was maintained at the new property by Sir William's son, another Sir William, who employed six men purely for the purpose of carrying him and his drunken guests to bed after parties. A committed Jacobite and a leader of the plotting for the 1715 rising, Sir William was MP for Newcastle and lost his enthusiasm for the cause after an arrest warrant was issued for him. A rather dissolute character, he died in 1728 leaving huge debts to the tune of £77,000 (almost £10 million today). Sir William had married in 1725, but he and his wife, Barbara Villiers, had no children and William left only an illegitimate daughter named Elizabeth Orde. As a result he left his estates to his nephew, Sir Walter Calverley, upon the condition that Sir Walter change his name to Blackett and married Elizabeth Orde.

Sir Walter agreed to this and inherited in 1728, along with his new wife. The couple chose to settle at Wallington and the 21-year-old Sir Walter Calverley-Blackett substantially remodelled the property (in Palladian style) and the grounds, forming the bulk of the magnificent house and estate which now survives.

After Sir Walter died in 1777, the estate passed to the Trevelyan family. One later resident was the naturalist and geologist Sir Walter Calverley Trevelyan who, with his wife, Pauline Jermyn, hosted scientific and literary parties and exhibitions at the hall and members of the Pre-Raphaelite Brotherhood were frequent visitors.

The interior of Wallington Hall is beautifully furnished with attractions including the desk at which Thomas Babington Macaulay, a close personal friend of the family, wrote his seminal *History of England*, eight huge murals depicting the history of Northumberland in the central hall and a large collection of antique dolls-houses. The hall sits in an estate of 100 acres consisting of rolling parkland, a wooded dene, an ornamental lake, lawns and a recently restored wall garden.

Wallington Hall (Glen Bowman CC BY 2.0 https://commons.wikimedia.org/wiki/File:Wallington_Hall_02.jpg)

Carved Dragon's Heads at Wallington (© Gail Johnson/Adobe Stock)

Visitor Information

Car – A1 north to Newcastle then 20 miles NW (A696, Airport/Ponteland
   road) and turn off on B6342 to Cambo.

A1 south to Morpeth (A192) then 12 miles west (B6343).

Address – Cambo, Northumberland, NE61 4AR.

https://www.nationaltrust.org.uk/wallington

CHAPTER 6

The Victorians and Early Twentieth-Century Northumberland

Although it is now seen as a primarily rural agrarian county, Northumberland was one of the cradles of the Industrial Revolution. During the nineteenth century a number of entrepreneurs, engineers and innovators ensured the county led the way in a number of fields including coal mining, the railways, shipbuilding, armaments and heavy engineering. Many of these innovators have since been largely forgotten.

Many of the industrial developments took place in the south of the county (many in what is now North Tyneside but was, until 1974, Northumberland). As the Victorian age began in 1837, Northumberland was the fifth largest county in England but the twenty-fourth largest in terms of population. Increasing industrialisation in the south east of the county had seen the growth of some communities from small villages to thriving towns. Bedlington, for example, was home to several iron works along the banks of the River Blyth, as well as several stone quarries producing grind and whetstones but was increasingly at the hub of the developing Northumbrian coalfield. These developments led to a 10–20 per cent increase in population from 1821.

Northumberland had been a leader in the coal mining industry since the previous century, with extensive coalfields in the south east of the county and around Newcastle-upon-Tyne. At Wylam in the Tyne valley in 1810 and 1812, the colliery owner Christopher Blackett used the enforced idleness of a strike to experiment with using a primitive steam engine to haul coal to the nearby docks. Encouraged by the results he asked his colliery engineer, William Hedley, to design an efficient engine. In 1813 Hedley, and his two helpers, built two engines of similar design and named them *Puffing Billy* and *Wylam Dilly*. The engines were very successful in their tasks with *Puffing Billy* continuing to serve at the colliery until 1862. The then-owner of the colliery, Edward Blackett, sold the engine to the

Patent Office Museum in London. *Puffing Billy* is still on display at what is now the Science Museum. *Wylam Dilly*, meanwhile, is currently on display at the National Museum of Scotland in Edinburgh. The two are the oldest surviving steam locomotives. It is sad that neither of these machines can be displayed in the region where they were built and operated, but in 2006 Beamish Museum built and ran a replica of *Puffing Billy* (a replica built in 1906 can be seen in the German Museum, Munich).

Puffing Billy was innovative in many ways and had a great influence on the future design of engines. One man who was influenced and intrigued by the design was local engineer George Stephenson and he utilised several of the earlier innovations in his work. The success of *Puffing Billy* and *Wylam Dilly* further encouraged other north-east colliery owners to look to steam power.

George Stephenson

George Stephenson was born at Wylam in 1781. His parents were too poor to be able to give their children an education and George, who was illiterate until the age of 18, secured work as an engineman at a local colliery using his wages to pay for night-classes. By 1804 George was married with a small child and had moved to Dial Cottage at West Moor (the cottage still exists and can be visited), near to where he then worked as a brakesman at Killingworth Pit. Tragedy entered George's life as he suffered the loss of his 3-month-old infant daughter in 1805 and his wife, who died of tuberculosis just a year later. He left his 3-year-old son, Robert, in the care of a local

George Stephenson (© orion_eff/Adobe Stock)

woman and moved to Scotland but returned a months later when his father was left blind after a colliery accident. He moved back to West Moor, worked at Killingworth once more, and lived with his unmarried sister and his son. In 1811 George offered to make repairs and improvements to the pumping engine at High Pit, Killingworth, and was so successful that he was immediately promoted to enginewright for the Killingworth collieries.

The self-educated Stephenson was typical of many of the Northumbrian innovators, as he applied himself to a variety of technologies. Stephenson was fully aware of the danger of explosions in collieries and began working on a safety lamp, despite his lack of scientific knowledge. Stephenson demonstrated his lamp in front of two witnesses in 1815, only to discover that another scientist, Humphry Davy, demonstrated another lamp of a different, but similar, design to the Royal Society just months later. Because of his lack of education combined with his strong Northumbrian accent, Stephenson was accused of having stolen Davy's idea. This was despite the fact that Stephenson had demonstrated his invention first. The reason for the doubt was largely that most of the members of the Royal Society found it hard to stomach, and even to believe, that a man from an uneducated background could have possibly come up with the idea. The Royal Society was firmly behind this and awarded Davy £2,000 for his invention. A local committee, however, exonerated Stephenson and awarded him £1,000, stating that he had been working on his own 'Geordie Lamp' separately from Davy. In 1833, a House of Commons committee greed with this and stated that Stephenson had equal claim to having invented the safety lamp. Davy and his followers, however, absolutely refused to believe this. The experience over the safety lamp left Stephenson with a deep and lasting distrust of London-based experts.

Stephenson had taken a keen interest in the development and use of steam engines in collieries in Leeds and at his birthplace of Wylam, and in 1812 he used static engines to increase efficiency at Killingworth. The Napoleonic Wars were raging at that time and corn prices were at an all-time high, so he managed to persuade the colliery owners that the replacement of horses with steam engines could save them money and increase efficiency. In 1814 he completed the construction of his first locomotive engine, which he named *Blucher*. Although *Blucher* was a success, Stephenson himself believed it saved little money but he used the design to develop his ideas for more efficient and powerful engines. Stephenson constructed approximately sixteen engines during his time at Killingworth and, together with William Losh, introduced several innovations including new rail joints and steam-spring suspension. Among the engines he went on to design was one which was built at Robert Stephenson & Co. and named *Killingworth Billy*. It was originally thought that this was a later design built in 1826, but research undertaken in 2018 shows that it was in fact built ten years earlier. The engine is available to view at the Stephenson Railway Museum on North Tyneside.

In 1821 Stephenson, assisted by 18-year-old son Robert, was contracted to work on the newly commissioned Stockton & Darlington Railway. For this large contract a new company, Robert Stephenson & Co., was established in Newcastle. Another partner in the contract was Michael Longridge, whose Bedlington Ironworks produced the wrought-iron rails at the 4ft 8½in gauge requested by Stephenson (this gauge became, and remains, the world standard).

With the success of the Stockton & Darlington Railway behind him, Stephenson next worked on the wildly successful Liverpool & Manchester Railway. His success on this high-profile project attracted a great deal of praise and fame. Although Stephenson was somewhat dogged by an overly cautious attitude, and by his casual forecasts of costs, the offers of work both at home and abroad poured in. In many ways, however, Stephenson's greatest legacy was the influence he had on the Industrial Revolution and on fellow engineers such as his son, Robert, his former assistant, Joseph Locke, and Isambard Kingdom Brunel. Because of his success he became known as the 'Father of the Railways', but his success also took him away from his native North East to Leicestershire and then Derbyshire. George Stephenson died at Tapton House, Chesterfield, in 1848. In 1862 a classical statue of George Stephenson was placed at the junction of Neville Street in Newcastle, near to the city's Central Station. The cottage in Wylam where Stephenson was born, and his former home at Dial Cottage, were open to the public and housed museums but, unfortunately, have both recently been closed.

George Stephesnon's Locomotive 'Rocket', 1829 (© Archivist/Adobe Stock)

The Bedlington Ironworks, which worked with Stephenson, was founded in 1736 by William Thomlinson but went through several owners before being taken over by Gordon & Biddulph of London in 1809; during their ownership the site entered a period of prosperity under the stewardship of Michael Longridge (a close friend of George Stephenson). During 1814 the works was responsible for producing many of the components for Stephenson's first locomotive, *Blucher*.

In 1819 the Ironworks signed a deal with the nearby colliery at Choppington to provide cheap coal to the works, provided the works paid for a wagonway to link the two premises. Longridge had read widely on the subject of rails and decided on malleable iron rails. The next year the Bedlington Ironworks took out a patent on these malleable iron rails, which proved key to the development of long-distance iron rail

Bedlington Iron Works (Public Domain)

tracks (a length of track from the original Stockton-Darlington railway is preserved in storage at Woodhorn Museum). This 2-mile long wagonway was a huge success and was key in influencing George Stephenson to utilise the Ironworks. The manufacture of these malleable rails was much speedier than the previous manual casting techniques and this proved to be an important factor in the growth of the railway.

In the first year of Victoria's reign the Ironworks experienced a number of successes, including the establishment of a locomotive works on the Bebside side of the river. The first locomotive to be produced here was named after Michael Longridge and was the first of some 150 to be built here. Although this was a success for the company it put them into direct competition with Robert Stephenson and relations remained tense. The locomotives produced included the engine which pulled the first passenger train to leave King's Cross in 1852, the first trains in Holland and Italy. Other engines were exported to Austria, Belgium, France, Germany, Holland, Italy and Persia. In 1850 the company had produced rails and castings for use during the Crimean War. Numerous British companies also placed orders with the firm but by 1852 the works was in trouble and it is believed that the last locomotive, the *Prince Albert*, was produced in this year; just three years later the works was closed. By then, competition from larger towns and cities was proving very trying and the Ironworks changed hands again in 1861, when it was taken over by Messrs Mounsey & Dixon. A tragic incident occurred in 1862 when Mrs Mounsey was killed during a tour of the works and, showing the growing importance of the local coal industry, the Ironworks were bought by Bedlington Coal Company in 1865; their stewardship of the works lasted just two years and the works was closed down due to the pressures of competition.

In 1959 many of the remaining structures were demolished to make way for a public park, Dene Park. Although little today remains in this lovely wooded river valley to show the one-time industrial importance of the area, there are some sights which can be explored during a walk (or cycle) through the park. The remains of the large weir which provided much of the water which powered the works can still be seen. It was originally a massive structure but was badly damaged and partially washed away in a flood during 1886. Crossing the Furnace Bridge (carefully as it is quite narrow) one finds a car-park which was once the site of the nineteenth-century Dene House, from which one can easily explore the parkland which reaches almost as far as the impressive Hartford Hall (built in 1807 and converted into a Victorian mansion during the 1870s before seeing use as a miners' rehabilitation centre and, now, as private housing. Proceeding up-river on the tarmac path from Furnace Car Park, one comes across the ruins of the weir and a modern statue of Janus. Around 50 metres north of this statue are the substantial remains of one of the kilns and some associated buildings.

Visitor Information
Car – the park is most easily reached via the A193 and is clearly signposted.
Bus – a number of Arriva bus services can also be used, stopping at Hartford Hall, Bedlington Front Street and beside the Bank Top Hotel; from here it is just a short walk.

William Armstrong, Cragside

The greatest of the Victorian Northumbrian innovators was probably William George Armstrong, the future 1st Lord Armstrong of Cragside. Armstrong was probably the most remarkable of the many Victorian entrepreneurs and scientists of nineteenth-century Northumberland and Tyneside. He began his career as a solicitor, but his first love had always been engineering and science. Born in 1810, the son of a wealthy corn merchant and former Mayor of Newcastle, Armstrong became a partner in a Newcastle law firm, married Margaret Ramshaw in 1835 and built their own home in Jesmond Dene.

Armstrong had been a sickly child and had spent a large portion of his childhood in and around the village of Rothbury for the good of his health. It was here that he developed a love of angling, spending days fishing on the River Coquet and its tributaries and becoming known as 'the kingfisher'.

Lord Armstrong (CC 4.0 https://commons. wikimedia.org/wiki/File:Sir_William_ George_Armstrong.jpg)

Eleven years into his career, his love of fishing would lead to him taking the decision to give up law and go into engineering. He was fishing on the River Dee in the Pennines when he noticed a waterwheel and realised how inefficient the mechanism was. This led him to design a water-driven piston engine which was used to power a hydraulic crane. In 1845 Armstrong was closely involved in improving the water supply for Newcastle-upon-Tyne and he suggested using the excess water to power such a crane on the busy quayside. So great was the success of the crane that a further three were quickly ordered. A year later Armstrong was elected as a Fellow of the Royal Society as a result of his amateur engineering work.

Emboldened by this success, Armstrong set up his own engineering company, W.G. Armstrong & Co., at Elswick, and orders for hydraulic cranes were brisk. Supplying cranes to buyers across Britain, the business expanded quickly. In its first year the company produced forty-five cranes and employed more than 300 men, but ten years later it was producing 100 cranes a year and employing 3,800 men. Armstrong, ever the innovator, branched out into bridge building and also invented the hydraulic accumulator (pressure storage reservoir in which a non-compressible hydraulic fluid is held under pressure that is applied by an external source. The external source can be a spring, a raised weight, or a compressed gas), and then the weighted accumulator.

In the mid-1850s Armstrong read about the difficulties with artillery which were being experienced by the British Army during the Crimean War and took the decision to invent a lighter, more mobile artillery piece. He wanted the gun to not only be light, but also to be highly accurate with a greater range than current field guns. Once again, Armstrong's ideas were revolutionary. He settled on a breech loading design, featuring a rifled barrel constructed of iron around a steel inner lining. Rather than firing a ball, the Armstrong gun would fire a shell. As a design test, Armstrong had a 5-pounder version of the gun built and tested it successfully. At the request of the government he then designed an 18-pounder version for official testing against several competitors.

After trials the Armstrong gun was declared by far the most effective and efficient gun, and in a shrewd and patriotic move, Armstrong voluntarily turned over the design patent to the government. This magnanimous gesture resulted in Armstrong being knighted and introduced to the Queen. He was also made the Engineer of Rifled Ordnance to the War Department and worked to update Woolwich Arsenal, while forming the Elswick Ordnance Company to manufacture weaponry for the British government.

It was at this stage that resentment against Armstrong, combined with old-fashioned attitudes among some of the forces, created a campaign against the revolutionary new gun. Many thought of Armstrong as a Northern interloper, while competitors were jealous that he was not an established weapons designer. In addition, many in the army (and some in the navy) remained rather hidebound and were not enthusiastic about the introduction of new and revolutionary technology. As a result of an extremely malicious campaign, which involved bad-mouthing Armstrong's designs and writing critical letters to the newspapers, orders dried up and the government ordered that all such guns would be produced at Woolwich, leaving Armstrong out of pocket. He did, however, secure an agreement allowing him to sell his guns to both sides in the American Civil War, while the British army went back to outdated muzzle-loading artillery. Armstrong also resigned his position with the War Office.

In the 1860s Armstrong turned his attention towards the design and manufacturing of naval guns. In collaboration with Tyneside shipbuilder, Charles Mitchell, Armstrong & Co produced its first warship, HMS *Staunch*, in 1868. One problem facing this new development was the old bridge across the Tyne, which restricted naval access to Elswick. Armstrong turned his fertile mind to the problem and, using his experience of hydraulics, designed the remarkable Swing Bridge which is still in use today.

The construction of the Swing Bridge encouraged Armstrong to expand and, in 1884, to build a shipyard at Elswick for the production of military vessels. The first vessels to be constructed were for the Austro-Hungarian navy, while the first battleship to be built at Elswick was the HMS *Victoria* three years later. One of Armstrong's best customers was Japan, and a large number of Elswick-built ships helped the Japanese destroy the Russian fleet at the Battle of Tsushima in 1905. It was said that every Japanese gun that fired on that day was built at Elswick.

At this time Elswick was the only place in the world where a battleship could be constructed and armed in the same location. However, Armstrong continued to develop other fields for the company and continued to build hydraulic engines and other products. So great was the success of the Elswick company that the population of Elswick increased from 3,539 in 1851 to 27,000 in 1871. In 1894 Armstrong won a lucrative contract to build and install the hydraulic engines which would power the iconic Tower Bridge in London.

Although Armstrong remained at the head of the company he had founded, in the 1860s he took the decision to leave some of the running of the company to a group of able appointees. Armstrong began to dedicate more time to landscaping the area around his Jesmond Dene house and contracted the architect John Dobson to build a banqueting hall in the Dene. Although the Armstrongs seem to have had a great liking for

Jesmond Dene, Sir William wished to build a house in the countryside allowing him to escape from the pressures of business.

In 1863 Armstrong returned to Rothbury, buying a parcel of land in the narrow valley of the Debdon Burn. After the land was cleared Armstrong supervised the construction of a relatively simple house, which he called Cragside, while he and his wife oversaw the planting of a variety of trees and mosses. The house would undergo lengthy alterations throughout the remainder of the century and so great were the improvements that a witness in the 1890s described the house as the 'palace of the modern magician'.

By 1869 Armstrong had decided to make Cragside his primary home and he hired architect R. Norman Shaw to transform the simple house into something much grander. The transformation of Cragside took place over the next thirty years and in Armstrong's own words became his 'very life'. Armstrong and Shaw generally had a good relationship, although Shaw was tested by Armstrong frequently changing his ideas, leading to the house lacking an overall unity. Nevertheless, Cragside became, according to Pevsner, 'the most dramatic Victorian mansion in the North of England'.

Cragside House (© Peter Claxton/Adobe Stock)

A classic example of the Tudor Revival style, Cragside remains one of the most beautiful and unusual Victorian country houses in Britain.

Typically, Armstrong insisted on adding labour-saving and innovative devices into his property. The kitchen, for example, has a hydraulically powered dumb waiter and spit, while dinner guests were summoned by an electric gong. Given his fascination with water it is no surprise that Armstrong also arranged for a Turkish bath to be installed.

Armstrong also used Cragside to showcase his impressive art collection and to entertain a wide range of guests. Among these guests were his foremost customers, including the Japanese Emperor, various dignitaries, and a visit by the Prince and Princess of Wales.

One of the most remarkable rooms in this remarkable house is the drawing room. Designed in a far more opulent and Renaissance style, this beautiful room features a top-lit ceiling and Jacobethan plasterwork, but the attention of most visitors is taken by the massive and remarkable inglenook fireplace. Built of marble, the fireplace is said to weigh 8 tons and to be the biggest inglenook in the world.

Unsurprisingly, Armstrong also wished to feature technological innovations in the grounds of his house. He supervised the creation of no fewer than five lakes on the estate and used the water from these lakes to power a number of hydraulic machines and mechanisms. In 1868 Armstrong installed a hydraulic engine followed by a Siemens dynamo, creating the world's first hydroelectric power station and using it to power various devices in the house and on the estate. This led to Cragside becoming, in 1880, the first home to be powered by hydroelectricity. Armstrong continued to innovate with devices in the house including a dishwasher, vacuum cleaner and a washing machine. In the gardens the conservatory featured an electrically powered self-watering system which also turned the plants so that they had an equal supply of light.

One of the main attractions of Cragside is the stunning scenery of the estate in which it sits. Armstrong's wife, Margaret, oversaw much of the extensive planting and landscaping work. There is an extensive rock garden below the house featuring many rare alpines, and the estate became famous for its massive collection of rhododendrons (one of which was named after Lady Margaret). The estate also possesses a large and varied collection of

Cragside House by Gail Johnson (© Gail Johnson/Adobe Stock)

coniferous trees including the tallest Scots Pine in Britain. It is reputed that the Armstrongs oversaw the planting of more than 7 million trees at Cragside and it is a fact that the replanting slightly altered the climate of the surrounding area. As Cragside House took shape, Armstrong continued to expand his estate so that by the 1880s the grounds consisted of 1,700 acres and his wider estate in the Cragside area consisted of 15,000–16,000 acres. Many of the farms benefited from machinery powered by hydroelectricity.

Today Cragside is owned and looked after by the National Trust with the grounds and house open from mid-February through to mid-December (last admission is at 4 pm (3 pm in November and December) while last access to the house is one hour before closing). The grounds are extensive and contain over 30 miles of footpaths, access for vehicles and lakeside walks. Among the attractions in the grounds are a rhododendron maze, waterfall, play area, numerous picnic sites and a trail where the whole family can test their agility. The original powerhouse beneath the dam wall contains a whole host of educational materials while the visitor centre also boasts educational attractions, a gift shop and café. The grounds are one of the last bastions in Britain of the red squirrel, while other wildlife abounds in the beautiful forested grounds. A more recent

The Iron Bridge at Cragside (timsaxonphoto) (© timsaxonphoto/Adobe Stock)

attraction is the recently installed 17-metre long Archimedes Screw which has restored hydroelectric power to Cragside House. The screw, powered by water from Tumbleton Lake, provides sufficient electricity to power all of the 350 light bulbs in the main house.

Guests can even stay at Cragside with two holiday cottages available. Park Cottage is a south facing spacious three-bedroom property with beautiful views over the Coquet Valley and the Simonside Hills, while Garden Cottage is the original home of Lord Armstrong's agent and enjoys superb views over the Italian Terrace and historic parkland, with the Coquet Valley and Simonside Hills beyond. A bunkhouse converted from two woodland workers' cottages is also available, and sleeps sixteen. Anyone interested in staying in one of the properties at Cragside should contact the National Trust via the Cragside House website: https://www.nationaltrust. org.uk/cragside/features/holiday-at-cragside.

The nearby village of Rothbury provides an ideal location to explore both Cragside and most of Northumberland. The village itself is both picturesque and busy with a number of very interesting shops and galleries. The village is a haven for wildlife lovers, artists and photographers and is very welcoming to visitors. One of the most popular attractions for visitors is a visit to Rothbury Family Butchers at Townfoot (the main street at the east end of the village). There are numerous places to stop in Rothbury including several hotels, B&Bs and a bunkhouse.

Visitor Information

Car – A697 (Morpeth – Coldstream road), 15 miles NW of Morpeth turn onto B6341 at Moorhouse crossroads. Entrance to Cragside is 3 miles on left. There are free car parks throughout the estate. Sat-nav: please note that sat-navs sometimes try to bring drivers in through the exit, please ignore sat-nav and follow brown signs for entrance.

Bus – Arriva service X14 runs from Newcastle to Rothbury (via Morpeth) every day although there is a 15 minute walk or a taxi journey needed from Rothbury (see Arrive NE website for timetables).

Address: Rothbury, Morpeth, Northumberland, NE65 7PX

Grace Darling, Northumbrian Heroine

In September 1838 an unassuming 23-year-old Northumbrian woman became a national celebrity and Victorian Britain's greatest heroine. Grace Horsley Darling was born at Bamburgh in November 1815. Her parents, William and Thomasin, had a large family and Grace was the second youngest of nine children (four boys and five girls). Grace was only weeks old when her parents took her and the rest of the family to Brownsman Island in the Farne Islands. Her father was lighthouse keeper, but in 1826 they relocated to Longstone Island when the lighthouse was also moved. Although the housing conditions at their new home were better than on Brownsman, little could be grown on Longstone and this meant that Grace's father had to make frequent trips by rowing boat back to their former garden to harvest vegetables and tend to their animals.

Although Grace never attended school, her father educated her in reading, writing, arithmetic, geography and history. She was also educated on the scriptures and on the old tales of the border. Her father was strict but well-loved and Grace appears to have been something of a favourite. The family were very musical. Her father sang and played several instruments as well as writing his own songs. Grace obviously appreciated this as she developed a reputation for having a fine singing voice. As her brothers and sister grew up and moved away, Grace became assistant keeper to her father and was responsible for caring for her ageing parents. She seems to have excelled in both of these roles and worked well with her father.

In the early hours of 7 September 1838, Grace looked out of an upstairs window and saw that a paddle steamer, the SS *Forfarshire*, had run aground on the half submerged rocky island of Big Harcar. There was a fierce storm at the time and conditions were extremely poor. The ship had run aground earlier that night and had broken in half; her stern section was submerged, leading to the death of a number of passengers and crew. Grace quickly alerted her father and after assessing the weather he declared that it was too rough for the nearest lifeboat (at Seahouses) to put out. The two decided that they would attempt a rescue themselves using the family's 21ft Northumberland

Grace Darling by Thomas Musgrave Joy (Public Domain)

coble. Grace and her father rowed the coble along the leeward side of the island, a distance of almost a mile. Upon reaching Big Harcar they determined that a small group of survivors had taken refuge on the rock. Grace's father helped the four men and one woman, Mrs Sarah Dawson, into the coble while Grace held the rowing boat steady. Her father and three of the male survivors rowed the coble back to Longstone, and Grace remained there to aid in looking after the survivors while her father rowed back to rescue a further four survivors.

Despite the conditions the Seahouses' lifeboat had put out to sea, with one of Grace's brothers, William Brooks Darling, as one of the crew. Upon arriving at Big Harcar the lifeboat found only the bodies of Mrs Dawson's two children and a clergyman. The weather was now so poor that the lifeboat could not be taken back to Seahouses and instead put in to Longstone. The storm continued and the lifeboat crew and survivors were forced to remain on Longstone for the next three days.

There were only eighteen survivors from the sixty-four people the SS *Forfarshire* had been carrying. The Darlings had rescued nine of these while another nine had been swept out to sea in a lifeboat and were picked up by a passing vessel.

When the survivors did eventually reach the mainland, reporters from local newspapers quickly gleaned the story from them. One journalist from the *Berwickshire and Kelso Warder* interviewed the survivors and reported how one of them wept as he explained how he had been rescued by a young woman in a rowing boat.

In the days and weeks that followed, the news of Grace's part in the rescue spread far and wide with accounts being given in the local and national press. *The Times* carried a detailed account of the rescue and this provoked a great deal of correspondence with one writing to the newspaper asking: 'Is there in the whole field of history, or of fiction even, one instance of female heroism to compare for one moment with this?' There were poems written in her honour and testimonies to her courage and virtue. The Royal National Institution for the Preservation of Life from Shipwreck (later the RNLI) awarded Grace and her father with their Silver Medal. Awed supporters raised over £700, equivalent to over £550,000 today, for Grace, with Queen Victoria herself donating £50 to the fund. Her portrait, along with that of her father, was painted more than a dozen times, while Grace also received hundreds of letters praising her and many gifts. Rather more bizarrely, she even received several proposals of marriage.

Among the works which popularised Grace Darling's rescue was one, *Grace Darling, or the Maid of the Isles,* written by Jerrold Vernon. This was a highly fictionalised account which lacked accuracy but also created the legend of Grace as 'the girl with windswept hair'.

Grace was inundated with letters from admirers and received requests for her signature, a lock of her hair and even requests for her to kiss the letter and return it. As many young women might be, Grace was at first flattered by this attention and replied to each letter but the attention quickly became trying as her new-found fame showed no sign of declining. Indeed, her fame had spread beyond the shores of Britain with accounts being published and attracting praise across Europe, America and even Japan and Australia. The Duke of Wellington, in his capacity as Master of Trinity House, and effectively William Darling's employer, read the accounts and asked William to provide an account to him personally, while Longstone became a favourite site for tourists who would ask to speak to Grace, to touch her, or simply to see what this national heroine looked like. As descriptions of Grace's ordinary yet feminine appearance spread, this attracted the interest of many artists.

Unfortunately, neither Grace nor her family were particularly worldly-wise and not every seeming well-wisher had the best interests of Grace at heart. Just two months after the rescue Grace received news from Edinburgh circus owner, William Batty, that he was going to donate the takings from one of his nightly performances to her. Days later his agent arrived at Longstone and presented Grace with £20, telling her it was from the people of Edinburgh and inviting her to attend one of the performances. Grace agreed that she would do so as a way of thanking Mr Batty and the people for their kindness.

Batty, however, had promised the people of Edinburgh an appearance from the national heroine and was using his 'kind gesture' to boost his own profits. The news that Grace was going to appear in a circus appalled many of the respectable ladies in Edinburgh who were at that very time raising funds for her. In a letter they warned her not to appear telling her that it would turn the public against her, as they would believe she was courting publicity and exhibiting herself in order to gain monetarily. Appalled by this revelation, Grace was said to have wept when she received the letter. Grace realised she had been very naïve and felt guilty over the ill-feeling it was causing. Her father wrote to the newspapers informing them that Grace had no intention of appearing at the circus and that she would not court publicity and popularity. Grace became increasingly concerned over her new-found fame, and the role placed upon of her of a national heroine sat uneasily. Along with this came the additional pressure of the wealth which had come to Grace from well-wishers. The Darling family was unused to this level of wealth.

The Darling family, and Grace in particular, found unlikely friends in the Duke and Duchess of Northumberland. Shortly after the Batty affair Grace and her father were asked to visit the duke at Alnwick Castle. The Darling family had a relative who owned a greengrocers' shop in Narrowgate in

Alnwick and the Darlings often visited. When they arrived to be presented to the duke, the people of Alnwick had heard the news and lined the streets to welcome Grace and her father. The duke had already met the Darlings during a visit to Longstone and he had taken a keen interest in the rescue, even going so far as to write to the Duke of Wellington to alert him to the courage shown by Grace and her father. Once they arrived at the castle they were met with a warm welcome from the duke and duchess and were presented with two medals which had been struck especially for the occasion, while the duchess presented Grace with a shawl. The Duke of Northumberland took it upon himself to offer to become a self-appointed head of a trust to look after this money and practically as a guardian for Grace. His concern for the family was genuine, he was aware of the Batty affair and realised that the Darlings could do with assistance. This meant that the quite large sums of money which were being donated to Grace would henceforth be channelled through the duke's lawyers. Grace's father, William, was appreciative and supportive of the offer. The duke also appointed three trustees who were all known to the Darlings, being Crewe Trustees from Bamburgh.

Grace had obviously learnt from the Batty incident, and when the manager of the Adelphi Theatre in London offered her £10 per week to appear in a production entitled *The Wreck at Sea*, she politely declined. Other similar invitations came from a number of other London theatres but all were declined, as was the rather bizarre offer to have Grace display herself as an exhibition in the capital. In her letters of rejection, Grace often said that the successful rescue was not down to her and her father's actions, but to the grace of God.

The duke maintained contact with the family and at Christmas in 1838 he sent a number of gifts to the family, including a gold watch for Grace, prayer books, a silver teapot and, perhaps most useful of all, sets of the newly invented Charles MacIntosh waterproof clothing. In the next year the duke personally financed the building of a lighthouse on Coquet Island and recommended Grace's brother William (who had been on the Seahouses lifeboat) as keeper.

The duke took his role as guardian seriously and corresponded with Grace on a regular basis with the warmth of the relationship coming across in the letters. In one such letter the duke said he had heard that Grace's brother, William, had married and asked her if she was thinking of marriage. Grace replied that she had not accepted any of the many proposals she had received because she had heard that in a marriage the man was the master, and she had heard many tales of bad masters.

In the years following the rescue the fame did not die down and Grace continued to be regarded as a national heroine. This, increasingly, was much to her dismay as she became more and more uncomfortable with the trappings of fame and celebrity. Among the marriage proposals she turned down were several from men with substantial titles but, increasingly, Grace wanted to return to her previously uncomplicated and quiet life and this was one of the reasons for her refusing to accept a suitor. As the fame continued the unwanted intrusions into her life began to take their toll.

The invitations became a source of irritation to Grace and she declined, against her father's wishes, an invite by the Lord Mayor of Newcastle to attend a private function where money from a subscription fund would be presented to her. In 1841 a request was made by a group of Hull ladies to attend the opening of a bazaar to raise funds for shipwrecked mariners (the SS *Forfarshire* had sailed from Hull), but she once again declined. The committee was overly persistent, writing to Grace six times, hinting that Queen Victoria might attend, and saying that because the SS *Forfarshire* had sailed from Hull she should oblige them by visiting. Finally, Grace wrote back saying that the Duke of Northumberland, in his capacity as her guardian, had advised her to have all future letters forwarded to him. Still the letters came and eventually Grace took the difficult decision to ignore them, although she felt that she was perhaps offending people. It had become clear that Grace possessed a strong sense of faith, but even this led to increased stress as many clergymen wrote to her asking to meet with her to reflect on spiritual matters. This greatly troubled Grace as she feared that they were attempting to make her into some form of icon of the faith. Once again she fell back on her guardian and by this stage it was clear that she was increasingly relying on the duke to protect and shelter her from the never-ending stream of letters and visits.

By 1842 even Longstone was no longer providing protection and privacy. One of her sisters had become a widow and had moved back with her daughter, then one of her brothers was appointed as deputy to her father and moved in with his family. Furthermore, building work to construct cottages was taking place on the island at the time. Feeling in need of a break she visited her brother on Coquet Island, but was still hounded when she sailed from Seahouses. After this she visited her cousins in Alnwick but was caught in a storm on the way and soaked. Upon her return to Longstone it seemed that she had caught a virus during this excursion and she developed a persistent cough which refused to clear. Throughout that summer of 1842 Longstone continued to attract visitors hoping to catch a glimpse of Grace and, tiring of the attention, she began to shun outside activities.

Grace had been a strong young woman but now began to weaken visibly. After becoming increasingly weak her family decided to move her to the fresh country air of Wooler and she recovered temporarily here, but on moving in to the narrow confines of her cousins' house in Alnwick she declined rapidly. The Duchess Charlotte became aware of this and had Grace moved to a larger townhouse in a quiet part of the town. The Duchess visited Grace but this kind gesture caused only distress, with Grace beginning to have nightmares about staring eyes following her and believed that everyone was constantly trying to find fault with her. Attempts to ease her anxiety failed and the Percy family's physician diagnosed tuberculosis.

The family took the decision to move Grace to Bamburgh where her sister, Thomasin, lived. However, the constant intrusion of well-wishers caused even more anxiety to Grace and she was moved to a box-bed with a sliding panel so that she could hide herself away. It was clear by this point that Grace was dying, but she never complained of the ravages of her illness as she was visited by her mother and remaining family. On the evening of 20 October 1842 Grace asked her father to lift her from her pillow and she died in his arms, aged just 26.

Grace was buried in a modest family plot in St Aidan's churchyard, Bamburgh, four days after her death. In death, as in life, Grace attracted publicity and the press reported that Bamburgh was full of mourners, rich and poor, many of whom had journeyed considerable distances. Her coffin was carried by four Bamburgh men and ten of her family followed.

Tomb of Grace Darling (© Paul/Adobe Stock)

There was also an intriguing mystery. The press reported that her family was accompanied by a young man from Durham wearing a black armband. It is thought that this man was a portrait painter named George, with whom Grace had secretly corresponded (it was also rumoured that one portrait painter had asked Grace to marry him). Although her burial place was marked only by a modest grave, an impressive monument was erected in the churchyard and this continues to attract visitors. On Inner Farne a stone was erected in St Cuthbert's Chapel commemorating Grace.

It took only days for a fund to be started for a memorial to Grace. Two years after her death a canopied Portland-stone memorial was installed featuring a life-sized carving of Grace lying next to an oar. The memorial was placed at the west end of the churchyard so it would be visible to passing ships. This memorial, however, did not weather well and it was replaced with one of Northumberland stone donated by Lord Armstrong from his estate at Cragside. Ironically, in 1893 a violent storm destroyed the canopy and it was replaced with a more ornate version. The old Portland-stone carving was placed within the church. Grace now lies in the modest family plot alongside her parents, her sister Thomasin and her brother Job.

The death of Grace shocked many and plunged a large number of admirers into mourning. The year following her death William Wordsworth wrote the poem *Grace Darling*. Tributes to Grace Darling have continued since her death with the latest being a 2018 historical fiction novel by Hazel Gaynor entitled *The Lighthouse Keeper's Daughter*.

Grace Darling Museum

The excellent Grace Darling Museum is run by the RNLI (Royal National Lifeboat Institution) and explores Grace's life from her childhood through the events of the rescue and to her death at a tragically young age. The museum houses a large number of personal items, letters and portraits, along with the actual coble boat which was used by Grace and her father during the rescue. There is also a fabulous model of the Longstone lighthouse which was for so many years Grace's home and audio-visual tools guarantee the visitor an immersive and fascinating visit. The museum was originally opened a century after the rescue and in 2016 and 2017 the museum was awarded a rosette for quality assured visitor attractions by Visit England.

Directions

The museum is situated in the middle of the village of Bamburgh, opposite St Aidan's Church and a short walk from Bamburgh Castle.

Car – from the A1 turn off onto the B1341 and follow the signs for Bamburgh. There is a large car park at Bamburgh Castle.

Bus – Arriva service X18 runs regularly between Newcastle and Berwick and calls at Bamburgh with the bus stop being just a short walk from the museum.

Train – Berwick-upon-Tweed is the closest station.

Address

RNLI Grace Darling Museum, Radcliffe Road, Bamburgh, Northumberland, NE69 7AE.

Grace Darling Website www.gracedarling.co.uk

Telephone: 01668 214910

E-mail: askgracedarling@rnli.org.uk

Opening Times

April – September: open daily, 10 am – 5 pm

October – March: Tues – Sun, 10 am – 4 pm

Admission

Free

Emily Wilding Davison, Northumbrian Martyr

In October 1872 a young baby girl was born at Roxburgh House, Greenwich, SE London. Her parents were Charles Davison and Margaret Davison (née Caisley) and Emily was the third of the couple's four children. The family arrangement was quite odd as her father was a 45-year-old former merchant with experience in India, while her mother was the family's former housekeeper and was aged just 19. The two were linked by distant family bonds. Emily grew up in a mixed household with her siblings, parents and several of her nine half-brothers and sisters. She had a fairly privileged childhood, although it was shaped by the death of her younger sister, to whom she was closest, in 1880. This sister was only aged 6 when she died of diphtheria, contracted as a result of poor sanitary conditions in their new house.

Emily was well educated and, after some home-schooling, attended Royal Holloway College in 1891 in order to study literature. Unfortunately, the family finances were now in crisis with her father having made some poor investments in the tram business. The situation was exacerbated in 1892 when he died suddenly and Emily was forced to withdraw from education. Emily's mother subsequently moved back home to Northumberland and opened a small bakery and shop in the village of Longhorsley, just north of Morpeth. Emily and her mother had extensive connections in Morpeth and it is known that Emily had at least forty cousins living in or near the small market town.

After giving up her education Emily took on a job as a governess and used some of her wages to continue studying at evening classes. She eventually managed to save enough to fund a course at St Hugh's College, Oxford, and achieved a 1st class honours in English, but could not graduate due to Oxford refusing to grant degrees to women. After leaving Oxford Emily took on a number of teaching and governess jobs, but does not seem to have settled in any of these; in 1902 she began studying at the University of London from where she graduated in 1908.

Emily had always possessed a fiery and determined character with a firm belief in the need to fight against social injustice and was influenced by the growing suffragette movement during the early 1900s. In 1906 she joined the Women's Social and Political Union (WSPU) and quickly embraced their militant tactics to secure the vote for women. A fiercely independent woman, Emily railed even under the restrictions of the radical leadership of the WSPU.

In March 1909 Emily took part in a march of WSPU members to confront the prime minister. The march ended in a confrontation with the police and scuffling broke out, during which Emily was arrested and charged with assaulting the police and sentenced to one month in prison. Just months later Emily and two other suffragettes were arrested for interrupting the Chancellor of the Exchequer during a men-only meeting. Emily was sentenced to two months imprisonment as a result although she was released after a few days after she went on hunger strike. In September she was again arrested after throwing stones at the windows of a room where another men-only political meeting was taking place. Again she was sentenced to two months, but released after a few days following a hunger strike. Just weeks later she was arrested again following an attempt to throw stones at a cabinet minister, but was released without being charged.

Emily was arrested yet again for throwing stones at the minister, was sentenced to one week's hard labour and again went on hunger strike, but this time she was force-fed in a torturous, horrific, experience. Following her first experience of being force-fed Emily barricaded herself into her cell, but the authorities turned a fire hose on her resulting in her having to be taken to the infirmary to be warmed with hot water bottles before being once more force-fed. Labour politician Keir Hardie asked questions about this in the House and Emily successfully sued the authorities over the incident.

Davison continued her campaign during the next year and following the collapse of the Conciliation Bill and the rough treatment of a large body of suffragettes in early 1910, Emily was once again arrested after breaking windows at the Crown Office. She was once again imprisoned and force-fed.

The suffragette movement attempted to mount a widespread campaign in April 1911 when they attempted to avoid being entered on the census. Emily hid in the Houses of Parliament but was found and arrested, although not charged. As a result, Emily appeared in the census twice, once at her lodgings where her landlady entered her name, and once at the Houses of Parliament where the Clerk of Works entered her name.

Alongside her radical campaigning Emily also wrote a large number of letters to the press attempting to put across the WSPU's position and arguments in a non-violent manner, but she became increasingly convinced that self-sacrifice, possibly even involving the loss of life, might be required for the cause.

Between 1911 and 1912, Emily was arrested and imprisoned several times for arson attacks on post boxes. These attacks were a sign of Emily's increasing radicalism and were unauthorised by the WSPU leadership, with whom she had fallen out. In June 1912 Emily was in Holloway Prison on hunger strike and being force-fed when she decided to throw herself from one of the balconies with the belief that her death might influence the authorities to stop treating her fellow suffragettes in such a cruel manner. Emily survived the attempt but was badly injured, suffering two broken vertebrae and a severe head injury. Despite this the authorities once again force-fed her within days of her suicide attempt. Later in the year Emily was arrested for the final time when she mistakenly attacked a minister with a horse whip after mistaking him for David Lloyd George. Once again, she was imprisoned, went on hunger strike and, for the forty-ninth time, was force-fed.

On 4 June Emily Widling Davison purchased a return ticket in order to travel to Epsom along with the massive number of racegoers who were going to attend the Derby. Emily followed the day's racing and then before the big race she positioned herself close to the rail on the Tattenham Corner which was the final bend before the home straight. The leading group of horses having passed Emily ducked under the rail and walked onto the course avoiding at least one oncoming horse before appearing to reach up to the bridal of the King's horse, Anmer. The horse, with jockey Herbert Jones aboard, had no chance of avoiding her and careered headlong into Emily.

Emily was knocked backwards for 30 metres and some reports claim that Anmer kicked her in the head, but this is unproven and the attending surgeon denied it, while Herbert Jones was unseated and dragged for a short distance. Both Emily and Jones were knocked unconscious immediately. Crowds rushed onto the course to provide medical aid with Emily being taken to a nearby cottage hospital. Emily had an operation two days later to relieve pressure on the brain and lay unconscious for a further two days, during which she received hate mail, before she succumbed to her injuries, the most serious of which was a fracture at the base of the skull. Among her effects were found two WSPU flags which she had tacked into the back of her coat, her railway ticket, a ticket to a suffragette dance for later that day, her race card and a diary which had appointments for the following week listed in it.

An inquest into Emily's death established a verdict of death through misadventure, determining that Emily died as a result of being accidentally knocked down after deliberately invading the racecourse. The coroner refused to bring a verdict of suicide due to a lack of evidence. The WSPU immediately began to build up a campaign to turn Emily Wilding Davison into a martyr for the cause of suffrage while the press at the time tended to be unsympathetic.

On 14 June Emily Wilding Davison's body was taken from Epsom to London. The WPSU had organised things quickly and efficiently. Her coffin was escorted by an estimated 5,000 suffragettes along with hundreds of male supporters. A procession through part of London followed with 50,000 people lining the streets. Although there were some protests and reports of bricks being thrown at the coffin, most of the crowd seemed to be respectful. In a carriage behind were Emily's close family. These included her mother, Margaret, sister Letitia (now Madame de Baecker), half-brother Captain Henry Davison, a cousin, Mrs Lewis Bilton (formerly Jessie May Caisley) and a Miss Morrison. Some reports described Miss Morrison as an intimate companion of Emily, hinting at a relationship, but she is likely to have been a relative who had acted as a companion to Emily when she had spent time with her mother at Longhorsley. Following a brief service at St George's in Bloomsbury, the coffin was taken to King's Cross and thence by train to Newcastle. At many of the stops the train halted to allow crowds to pay their respects.

The next morning the coffin was taken to Morpeth, where the Davison burial plot lay in St Mary the Virgin Church. When the train carrying Emily's coffin arrived at Morpeth it took over an hour to remove the many wreaths which had accompanied it. A massive crowd, estimated at 20,000, crowded the streets of the picturesque market town. After Emily's coffin arrived at St Mary's, the Benwell Silver Band played *La Marseillaise*. The people who crowded the streets of Morpeth were uniformly respectful to the occasion with the *Northern Echo* reporting that the crowd was 'becoming and decorous'.

At the insistence of Emily's mother, who was no doubt devastated by her daughter's death, the coffin was handed over to the family upon

Emily Davison's Funeral in Morpeth (Public Domain)

Emily Davison c. 1910-1912 (Public Domain)

arrival at the church where her male cousins took over as pallbearers. Just three local suffragettes were permitted entry into the churchyard for what was described as a private service. These three folded the banner, reading 'Welcome Home, Northumberland's Hunger Striker', which had welcomed Emily home to Northumberland and it was placed on her coffin. Emily's gravestone in the quiet churchyard is inscribed with the motto 'Deeds not Words', the slogan of the WPSU.

As described by Maureen Howes in her account of the life of Emily, the family of the fallen suffragette conformed to a strict silence where Emily was concerned. They ignored the speculation and fevered accounts of Emily's life and tragic death. The extended family closed ranks and refused to answer any questions. Out of respect for Emily and her family they maintained this silence for many years as Emily's story took many twists and turns largely due to speculation.

St Mary the Virgin Church, Morpeth

Car or Train – parking is available in Morpeth and it is a short walk from the town centre of this charming market town. Alight from the train at Morpeth. Follow the A197 (with a short diversion through the lovely Carlisle Park and perhaps calling off to see the statue of Emily Davison in the park) Morpeth – Clifton road and the church is visible from the roadside.

Bus – Arriva services X14, X15, X16 and X18 all go directly past the church. Nearest stop is at the Sun Inn, just yards away.
St Mary the Virgin Church, Morpeth,
St Marys Field
Morpeth
Northumberland
NE61 2QT
01670 503326

The church also has a fine entrance to the churchyard (rumoured locally to have been built for the comfort of guards protecting against grave-robbers) and there are numerous Commonwealth War Graves Commission headstones. These include one for a Belgian soldier of the First World War, many Polish graves (largely of airmen from nearby RAF Morpeth) and Dutch graves (again of airmen) from the Second World War.

Emily Wilding Davison's Grave

Emily Wilding Davison's grave lies in St Mary the Virgin Churchyard in Morpeth. A recently unveiled statue of Emily stands in Carlisle Park in the centre of town. The church and grave are easily located and Morpeth is an ideal location for exploring Northumberland enjoying proximity to many historic sites while also having heritage sites of its own including a medieval castle and a medieval chantry which has been turned into a visitor information centre, craft shop and bagpipe museum.

Morpeth also enjoys excellent transport links being on the East Coast Mainline, lying just off the A1 and having regular bus links to Newcastle, Alnwick, Rothbury and Berwick.

Select Bibliography

Beckenstall, S., *Prehistoric Rock Art in Northumberland* (The History Press, Stroud, 2001)

Bowness, E., *The Photographer's Guide to Northumberland* (Long Valley Books, 2017)

Dixon, R., *Northumberland: off the beaten track* (Createspace, 2012)

Fraser, G. McD., *The Steel Bonnets: story of the Anglo-Scottish Border Reivers* (Harper Collins, 1989)

Hall, G., *Northumberland: including Newcastle, Hadrian's Wall and the Coast. Local, characterful guides to Britain's Special Places* (Bradt Travel Guides, 2019)

Percy, R., *Lions of the North: the Percys and Alnwick Castle. A Thousand Years of History* (Scala Arts & Heritage, 2019)

Tomlinson, W.W., *Comprehensive Guide to the County of Northumberland* (British Library, 2011)

Watson, G., *The Border Reivers* (Northern Heritage, 2017)

Websites

English Heritage: www.english-heritage.org.uk

Landmarks Trust: www.landmarktrust.org.uk

National Trust: www.nationaltrust.org.uk

Newcastle University (rock art group): www.rockartmob.ncl.ac.uk/main/res/pdf/LordenshawRAMP.pdf

Northumberland Coast Area of Natural Beauty: www.northumberlandcoastaonb.org.uk

Northumberland Tourism: www.northumberlandtourism.org.uk

Visit England: www.visitengland.com/things-to-do/northumberland

Visit Northumberland: www.visitnorthumberland.com

Index